JUDAISM
AND PRAYER

ISSUES OF FAITH

JUDAISM AND PRAYER

Growing Towards God

DR. HERBERT M. BAUMGARD

Rabbi, Temple Beth Am

South Miami, Florida

UNION OF AMERICAN HEBREW CONGREGATIONS

NEW YORK

THE UNION OF
AMERICAN HEBREW CONGREGATIONS
gratefully acknowledges a special grant of the
CENTRAL CONFERENCE OF AMERICAN RABBIS
to assist the Union in the publication
of this volume as part of an
experimental series of adult publications.

This book is dedicated to my wife
SELMA BAUMGARD
whose sympathy and patience
have been of immeasurable assistance

Editor's Introduction

Prayer has been an integral part of the Jewish way of life. The concepts and ideas about prayer and expressed in prayer, as well as the forms and the language of prayer, have changed. The Jew has prayed from time immemorial.

The Rabbis of the Talmud went so far as to suggest that Abraham instituted the daily morning service; Isaac, the afternoon service; and Jacob, the evening service (B'rachot 26b). While the synagogue, as a formal institution, only came into being after the Temple in Jerusalem was destroyed, the Levites had always chanted their prayers and psalms as part of the Temple ritual. The High Priest on the Day of Atonement offered prayer in behalf of himself, his family, the people of Israel, and all of humanity. When Solomon dedicated the first Temple, he proclaimed it to be a House of Prayer, not only for his fellow Jews but even for the "stranger" (I Kings 8:41). The prophet Isaiah echoed this thought when he said "For my house shall be called a house of prayer for all the nations" (Isaiah 56:7). Thus the Jew recognized prayer as a spiritual need of all men.

With the destruction of the Temple, the synagogue became the focal point of prayer, as well as the center of study and public assemblage. While the Jew can and does pray anywhere —at home, in the field, and even in the market place—the synagogue was the formal place in which the people gathered to pray every day, and, especially, on the Sabbath and the holidays. The Jew, according to the ancient tradition, was required to recite one hundred benedictions every day (Menachot 43b). There are special prayers for every occasion, happy as well as sad.

In this volume, Reverend Doctor Herbert M. Baumgard helps modern man, living in an ever changing dangerous world, to understand the nature of prayer, its meaning, purpose, and impact. Utilizing the various disciplines available to man in our age, the author discusses some of the misconceptions about prayer, as well as the true meaning and efficacy of prayer. He calls upon the traditions of Judaism and its liberal interpretations to demonstrate how modern man might make an effective use of prayer.

We are grateful to Rabbi Baumgard for sharing his views and convictions with the reader, and we can learn from the deep faith and spiritual values that are implicit in his writing. It is our hope that this essay will influence those who have never attempted to pray, will stimulate those who have stopped praying to begin anew, and will fortify those who are habitual "prayers," offering them new insights. Prayer has meaning for its own sake, but beyond this, the world needs the implementations of the ideals and values expressed in prayer. The implication of a prayer for peace, justice, freedom, truth, etc., is that those who utter the prayer are willing to dedicate themselves to realize these ideals to the utmost of their ability. Only then, are we sincere in our prayer; only then do we pray at all; only thus can we change ourselves and the world in which we live. In this manner, man becomes a co-worker with God in the continuing and perfecting of creation.

RABBI CHAIM ISRAEL ESSROG
*Director of the Department of
Adult Jewish Education*

Preface

In preparing the contents of this book, and in gathering the materials necessary for it, I have learned a great deal. I am grateful to the National Board of Adult Jewish Studies of the Union of American Hebrew Congregations and the Central Conference of American Rabbis for offering me the opportunity to write on so important a theme. The honor is not lightly regarded.

I am indebted to Rabbis Eric Friedland, Harold I. Krantzler, and Daniel Jeremy Silver, and to Mr. Leo A. Diamond, who read the manuscript and offered constructive suggestions for its revision. My special thanks go to Dr. Chaim I. Essrog, the editor, who has worked closely and faithfully with me these many months. My appreciation also goes to Mr. Lazare Grunberg, who did the proofreading, and to Mr. Ralph Davis, who not only designed the book, but who assumed full administrative responsibilities for its publication.

The book is an attempt to describe the meaningfulness of prayer for modern man. My early interest in the dynamic aspects of prayer, emphasizing the interaction between man and God, stems from my inspirational teacher, Dr. Henry Slonimsky, Dean Emeritus of the Hebrew Union College–Jewish Institute of Religion, New York City. His spirit is not absent from these pages.

HERBERT M. BAUMGARD
South Miami, Florida
August, 1964–Elul, 5724

Contents

JUDAISM
AND PRAYER

Introduction

WE SPEAK OF THE "GOD OF ABRAHAM, ISAAC, AND JACOB," SAID the Hasidic Rabbi,[1] because God appeared to each of our fathers in a distinct and individual fashion. Our teachers understood that the truly religious person arrives at his own understanding of God after much searching and endless effort. It follows from this that each one of us must come to prayer from a different vantage point. No two people may pray from precisely the same depth of need, or with the same understanding of God, or, perhaps, even in the same manner, yet, there is abundant evidence that the overwhelming majority of people do pray in some fashion, however irregularly.

In one sense, it is idle to ask, "Is prayer legitimate? Is it consistent with modern science and knowledge?" The universality of the disposition to pray, whether among the primitives of the jungle or among the sophisticated intellectuals of the western world, seems to indicate that the urge to pray is a response to one of man's deepest needs. In fact, the Hasidic Jews of Eastern Europe in the eighteenth century taught that prayer was both natural and involuntary. To them, prayer was a response from within man towards a "pull" from without, a response which man could not resist even if he wished to do so.[2]

The Hasidim did not have to "think" about the legitimacy or the efficacy of prayer. They understood it to be as much an essential part of man as is his biological urge. They spoke of man's need to pray in this fashion. "When God created the world, He invested a part of Himself (a spark) in everything that He created. These sparks now yearn to re-unite themselves with their source."[3]

In this sense, a prayer is the yearning of the divine spark within man to join itself to more of itself. We could say in less poetic language, prayer is the effort of the better part of our nature to enlarge upon itself. The Hasidic Rabbis put it this way, "Prayer *is* God," that is, the divine communing with the divine.[4]

We, in modern times, can hardly define prayer in more compelling terms. The symbolic imagery of our eighteenth century forebearers may embarrass us. We might find it difficult to say that prayer is a kind of spiritual magnetism operating in the world, wherein the divine source and its creatures participate in a mutual "pull" towards each other. Perhaps the language of an American psychologist-philosopher might express the thought in more acceptable terms for us. Wrote William James, "He (man) becomes conscious that this higher part (of his nature) is co-terminous and continuous with a *more* of the same quality, which is operative in the universe outside of him, and which he can keep in working touch with, and, in a fashion, get on board of, and save himself. . . ."[5]

The deepest insights of psychology and religion support each other in the understanding that man can tap infinitely deeper resources within himself than he habitually uses. Prayer is a way to the appropriation of these spiritual resources.

THE IMAGE OF GOD

Judaism has always taught that man is made "in the image of God." Prayer is our effort, voluntary or involuntary, to fill that image within us with greater content. It might be said that prayer is part of the process through which we grow towards the divine. Historically, Judaism has conceived of God as the source of love, justice, and mercy, the author of freedom.[6] When Jews pray, they pray towards this "image." We pray that we may be able to take more of these qualities into ourselves that we may become more God-like. To obtain more of the power of God for ourselves, means that we, through contemplation of the Divine, take more of love and justice and mercy into ourselves. In this process, we fill the spiritual image within ourselves with actuality. We make real the potential that was with us at birth, because we are created with this potential. The fact that we are created in the image of God does not mean that we are born "like God." It means that, with disciplined work, we can bring that image to fruit and flower.

The Rabbis, commenting upon the verse in Genesis, "Let us make man in OUR image,"[7] taught: God says to every man and woman, "Let US make man." That is, God says to the individual, "Let us together, you and I, create man, for, what you

4

do with yourself is a significant part of the creation."[8] Prayer, then, has to do with creation and building, the building of a better person.

THE PROCESS OF PRAYER

Some people think of prayer as mere verbalization. This cannot be. Sincere prayer has thought behind the words, but profound prayer requires even more. Life is not divided into compartments of thoughts, compartments of words, and compartments of deeds. They are part of each other, inextricably intertwined. He who regularly attempts to pray without prior thought or study, and he who verbalizes his thoughts, without the intent of using the answer to his prayer in his work and deeds, misunderstands the nature of prayer. Prayer is part of a process which includes study, thought, words, and directed action. A prayer, properly conceived, combines the past and the future in a dedicated moment of the present. The sensitive person will cull from the past man's highest conception of God. He will glean from the past man's noblest aspirations, and he will come to his present moment of dedication armed with this knowledge and feeling. The person in prayer will seek not only communion with God as spirit, he will understand that the prayer-moment is a moment for building. His thought and study of man's best achievements will lead him, in his moment of contemplating the Divine, to ask, "How, now, can I make myself in Your image? What must I do in my daily life to show what I have learned in this moment?" The prayer might even solicit the proper action in a specific situation. The important thing, however, is that the "prayer" understand that in his prayer he links himself, not only to God, but he links past and future. In a very real sense, the prayer moment becomes a moment in eternity. Its function, in the last analysis, is to fill the spiritual image of man with the divine qualities and to bring more of love, justice, and mercy into the deeds of men. In the disciplined religious person, in the creative, love-giving man or woman, it is difficult to tell where the thought and study begin, and where the word and deed end. Our Jewish tradition teaches that God is "He who says and does, ha-o-mar v'-o-se,"[9] He who would be God-like, is one who prays and *does*.

5

The Prophet Jeremiah spoke of God as the "M'kor Chaim, The Source of Life." The prayer of Jews has ever been an expression of their yearning for a larger, more satisfying life. People pray when they are not willing to accept defeat; when they are lonely and seek companionship; when they are weak and ill and seek better health; when they are fearful and want to be reassured; when they are guilt-laden and seek forgiveness. Those who pray, express their need and demand for a broader experience of life. Conceived in these terms, prayer is the foe of pessimism. It is a manifestation of that mind and spirit which refuses to accept a restricted view of life. Prayer is a way of saying, "I believe that the world was created in such a way that men can find fulfilment for their deeper longings. I want and shall seek my own fulfilment."

The Jew prays in the mood of the biblical affirmation of the goodness of life. Our Scripture teaches that this world is good, that man can realize his legitimate aspirations in his years on this planet. Judaism teaches that if evil seems triumphant, its victory is only temporary, and justice will prevail in the end. For the Jew, forgiveness is readily available from a merciful God who is concerned with the needs of man, and aware of man's imperfections. Our prayer, as Jews, wells up from the conditioning of a lifetime that we need not settle for an ugly, unjust, diseased, lonely life. We pray in the conviction that life can be expected to yield better answers to problems than the present situation may offer. Only the man who hopes—prays. As one poet has said, "Only men incredulous of despair beat upwards to God's throne."[10] It was Jehudah Halevi who wrote that the Jews, in spite of their experience of persecution, are "prisoners of hope—asire tikvah."[11] We are incurable "prayers."

PRAYING TOGETHER

We have attempted, thus far, to describe some of the "spiritual climate" which accompanies the Jewish understanding of prayer. We have said:

1. Prayer is the yearning of man's highest nature to join itself to a "more" outside of itself, to assimilate itself to this "image."

2. Man is made in the "image of God," only to the extent that he is born with the potential to make himself in that image, and this is our work as Jews. Prayer is part of the means we use to fill our inner being with more of the God-like qualities of love, justice, and mercy.

3. Prayer is part of a process which begins with thought and study, continues through contemplation and verbalization, and, ultimately, into deed.

4. The Jew prays in the mood that God created the world in such a way that it would provide reasonable answers to man's legitimate aspirations. He prays, then, for more of life, for those things that make the healthy experience of life both materially and spiritually rewarding. Prayer is, in this sense, a refusal to despair, an accent on hope.

We must add a major fifth point here at the conclusion of our Introduction. While Judaism recognizes the importance of personal prayer, it has always emphasized communal prayer. It has encouraged personal prayer, but, usually in the synagogue, in a setting where: a) other human beings are present, and, b) the reminders of the traditions are strong enough to set a framework for the prayer. Some kinds of prayer flow best when one is alone. The spontaneous prayer, expressing one's deepest emotional needs in a moment of crisis, should not, of course, be kept waiting until one is in the synagogue. It is equally true, that study and meditation, which partake of the nature of prayer, can frequently best be done when one is alone. Nevertheless, while Judaism encourages personal prayer, it educates most strongly towards group prayer.

An event recently published in our newspapers can help us understand one of the reasons behind this emphasis. A policeman in a western city shot and killed a young secretary, whom he did not know. When questioned as to his motivation, the policeman replied, "God told me to do it." What manner of God does one contact when he prays? It is a simple thing for the individual to believe that a voice from his own subconscious is the Divine voice. Judaism contends that there is a danger in uncontrolled personal prayer which can lead one away from God Himself. Recognizing the difficulties accompanying prayer, Judaism holds that even so personal a thing as man's communication with his Maker ought to be conducted within a certain framework. For us, if the "voice" speaks other than in terms of

7

love, justice, and mercy, it is not the voice of God. Prayer, as the vain projection of the self-centered individual, is not authentic. The prayer of the individual, Judaism teaches, must lead him back to his fellow man and to society. For this reason, it is best to pray regularly in the midst of people trying to direct themselves towards a society based on the divine-like qualities. For Jews, the form of prayer is almost as important as the content. We do not pray to a God suddenly born in a moment of crisis, we pray to the God who inspired Moses to seek freedom, and who taught Hosea the meaning of love. We pray to "The God of Our Fathers."[12]

I

Prayer Is Work — "Avodah"

A. SOME MISCONCEPTIONS ABOUT PRAYER

IN SPITE OF THE INCREASE IN THE ATTENDANCE AT RELIGIOUS services in America during recent years, it is fair to say that the majority of people today are rather confused about the meaning of prayer. It is a very common experience to hear a person who regularly attends worship services say, "I don't really understand what I am doing," or, "I am not certain to whom I am praying," or, "I do not know whether my prayer is answered or not."

The honest person will have some legitimate doubts as to the best way to commune with God. He will find difficulty in defining the image which is the object of his reaching. He will wonder whether the specific means he uses is appropriate, or whether the accepted means used by the community in public worship is adequate. He may well find it difficult to measure whether or not his prayer has been answered.

One of the reasons many of us find it difficult to pray is that we think of God in terms of an old man with a beard who sits up in the sky and runs errands for those who would make demands on Him. When our particular errand is not performed, we may wonder if we prayed properly, or whether God is really concerned about us. Some of us conclude that if God is not as our childhood dreams pictured Him to be, then, He has no existence at all. We moderns have been zealous in developing new scientific concepts, but we have been most unimaginative and uncreative where religion is concerned. Perhaps we have been downright fearful of doing original and profound thinking on the subject. For modern man to be able to pray with integrity, he must be able to conceive of a God-image which uses all the truths laboriously gleaned by men throughout the ages. In order to be religious, it is not necessary that we conflict with the highest knowledge that science has discovered. On the contrary, we must use every discovery, concerning both the nature of the physical world and the nature of man, to construct a religious view which will be the most consistent with reality and which will demand the noblest expression from us.

For example, it was once common to believe that man was a creature of small talents, and that he was merely the passive recipient of such power as God chose to distribute arbitrarily. Today, we tend to think of God and man as partners, interacting with each other in a creation that knows no end. The old emphasis on prayer is indicated in the petition, "God, help me." It may well be that the emphasis more consistent with reality should be, "God, help me to understand how I may work together with You to help myself."[1]

In preparing to write this book, I interviewed a number of people, and asked them if they prayed and how they prayed. I received many different kinds of replies, some startling, some amusing, and some spine-chilling. One man told me that he does not pray much now, but he used to pray sincerely when he was a lad. What did he pray for then? "I prayed when I came home later than the permitted hour," he said. "I prayed that my father would not whip me for violating his rule." This young man told me that if his father did not whip him, he knew that God had answered his prayer. The air is filled with prayers of a similar nature. Some people pray, "Oh, Lord, let me close this business deal. I need the money." Some girls pray, "Oh, Lord, let this boy fall in love with me." The embattled soldier prays, "Oh, Lord, let the enemy soldier be killed and not me." The perspiring prizefighter prays, "Oh, Lord, let me smash this guy into unconsciousness." Everybody "prays," including scoundrels and murderers, and it is clear that if God answered all prayers, the world would be a miserable place in which to live. Most people pray on the basis of surface whim and thought without weighing the motives that prompt them to pray. When God does not seem to answer a selfish, shallow, and sometimes cruel prayer, the petitioner may well exclaim, "There is no God!" Certainly, a part of that statement, at least, is true. We might say, *"Thank God, there is not that kind of God who will respond to the most ignoble of human wishes!"*

The prophet Isaiah, 8th century B.C.E., taught that a prayer prompted by greed and not motivated by ethical striving would not be answered. He proclaimed in the name of God,

> "When you spread your hands to pray,
> I will hide mine eyes from you . . .
> Yea, when you make many prayers,
> I will not hear
> . . . Wash you, make you clean,
> Put away the evil of your doings
> . . . Seek justice, relieve the oppressed . . ."
>
> (*Isaiah* 1:15–17)

Isaiah taught that the person who performed deeds of justice and compassion would find God waiting to communicate with him. A word which the Hebrews have used for prayer is *"t'filah,"* which comes from the verb which has been translated *"to judge oneself."*[2] Prayer involves self-judgment, self-improvement. It is a step towards the service of that which is holy and just, a path to the loving-giving life. Isaiah further teaches that if you have helped your neighbor in distress, if you have fed the hungry, clothed the naked, and aided those who are persecuted wrongly, if *then* you call, the Lord will answer you. If you cry for aid, He will say, *"Here I am!"* (Isaiah 58:6–9). It is but a summary of this teaching to say, when the man who strives for righteousness prays, he will be strengthened in his being and in his work. Are these not the legitimate goals of prayer?

B. THE ANSWER TO PRAYER IS "OF THE SPIRIT"

Our teachers have forcefully contended that God is not a genii who can be conjured up by the rubbing of a magic lamp. He is not a lackey who performs, without thinking, the will of the selfish and the unjust. Those who expect God to perform their every whim are merely projecting a power-hungry desire to command all things. Nor is God, in our tradition, a kind of benevolent storekeeper who cheerfully dispenses red bicycles and gold Cadillacs on demand. The essence of Jewish teaching is that God has given to mankind not only the physical world, which is capable of sustaining itself, but He has also given to man a creative self (nefesh)[3] which is capable of self-direction within broad boundaries and capable of infinite growth and renewal. Beyond this, Judaism contends, God does not dispense material gifts. He is "of the spirit," and His remaining storehouse consists

11

not of additional material things, but of the more precious gifts of courage, patience, and love. This kind of gift is accompanied by important reservations, however. The spiritual gift is something which has to be used by the recipient before it can show results! Many of us do not seek this kind of gift, because once we have it, we know that we must work at using it. Unfortunately, the thing many "praying people" want least to do is work. Let us understand the Jewish definition of prayer. The more ancient Hebrew word for prayer is "avodah"; the root meaning is "service-work." *There can be no value to prayer unless the one who prays is prepared to work and to use the gift of courage or strength, which he obtains from God, towards the solving of his problems.*

The classic example of God's answer to the lazy worshiper is described in the book of Exodus. The former slaves to Pharaoh once again demonstrated their lack of courage and their unwillingness to believe in their own free destiny, when they halted before the "Sea of Reeds" and demanded that Moses ask God for another miracle to overcome the obstacles before them. The text tells us that when Moses reluctantly prayed, relaying the request of the people, God replied, "Wherefore criest thou unto Me? Speak unto the children of Israel that they may go forward!" (Exodus 14:15.) A prayer cannot be an attempt to get God to do for us what we can and must do for ourselves; but a prayer for strength to do the task that lies before us is a legitimate prayer and can find its answer. There is a basic Hebrew prayer which goes,

> Adonai oz l'amo yiten
> Adonai y'varech et amo v'shalom
> May the Lord give His people strength
> May the Lord bless His people with peace.[4]

The prayer suggests that when we constructively apply our newly-found strength, we will attain to the "shalom," to the "peace" or to the "well-being," which we seek. It has been wisely said that he who rises from his prayer a better man, his prayer is answered.

II

"O Lord, How Can We Know Thee?"

O Lord, how can we know Thee? Where can
we find Thee? Thou art as close to us as breathing, and yet art farther than the farthermost
star.

(Union Prayerbook—p. 39)

A. THE MYSTERY BEYOND

WE ARE TOLD THAT THERE IS A BREATH-TAKING VIEW OF THE SEA
from a mountain road on the island of St. Thomas. There is a
sign there which reads:

LOOKOUT POINT
(Courtesy of Mountain Top Hotel)

In black pencil, below the lettering, is etched the addition,
"With a little help from God!" Man has almost succeeded in con-
vincing himself that he alone created the world. As we walk
down our city streets, which we have made into narrow corridors
walled up on each side with stone and metal, we find it difficult
to see the objects of nature, the sky, the sun, the stars, which
might remind us that the world is not the original work of man.
The leader of a certain nation said recently, "We shot a man
into the sky, too. What has God done that we haven't?" The
boast reflects an ignorance of the real nature of the sky. The
attention drawn to the moon by recent discoveries of human
beings has awakened a new interest in the secrets of space and
outer space. Inhabitants of the planet Earth have been forcefully
reminded that the moon is, after all, but a mere speck in our
solar system, and our solar system is but a small area in the
galaxy of which it is a part, while space seems to be the home of
an infinite number of galaxies. Each time man has made a con-
quest in the field of science, he has learned that the world, and

the universe, are much wider and deeper than he had ever before imagined. Each door we have opened leads but to many other doors. As man assembles more information, he learns that a full knowledge of the Creation becomes more difficult to grasp. As we open the door to the "heaven" in which we thought God resided, we find that this "heaven" is just a little box when compared to the greater truths beyond. *Each brilliant discovery of man leads but to a greater mystery.* The sensitive person stands before this mystery in awe and wonder. We have to be capable of this kind of wonder in order to be able to pray.

In our generation, no one was more informed about the physical laws undergirding our universe than Albert Einstein. He represents, perhaps, a pinnacle that man can hope to attain in intellectual and scientific accomplishment; yet, this "superman" wrote, *"The most beautiful thing we can experience is the mysterious. It is the source of all true art and science. He to whom this emotion is a stranger, who can no longer pause to wonder and stand rapt in awe, is as good as dead; his mind and eyes are closed. To know that which is impenetrable to us really exists, manifesting itself as the highest wisdom and the most radiant beauty which our dull faculties can comprehend only in their most primitive forms, this knowledge, this feeling, is at the center of true religiousness. In this sense, I belong in the ranks of devoutly religious men."*[1] Is not the combination of humility-adoration, which Einstein expresses here, the essence of the prayer mood?

B. THE FEAR (AWE) OF GOD

"To know that which is impenetrable to us really exists . . ." wrote Einstein, "this knowledge, this feeling, is at the center of true religiousness." This profound statement is based on the humility of a man who knew enough to know that all he knew was a mere detail compared with the total being of the universe. There is a saying attributed to a college professor which goes, "The more I know, the more I know there is to know." This willingness to admit that the most advanced human mind can comprehend only a small fraction of existence is the true beginning of wisdom. The message of our Bible, "The fear (awe) of the Lord is the beginning of knowledge" (Proverbs 1:7;

14

Psalm 111:10) is even more meaningful in our time of scientific discovery.

J. Robert Oppenheimer, while he served as Chief of the U.S. Atomic Research Project, was asked by TV's Edward R. Murrow on "Person to Person," "Mr. Oppenheimer, how did you feel when you exploded the first atomic bomb?" Mr. Oppenheimer, one of the world's outstanding physicists, replied, "My first response was one of fear; fear that this great secret, this great power potential existed all the time, and we were ignorant of it, and fear that other forces exist now with, perhaps, greater power, and we are ignorant of them also." Only the most educated and the most sensitive people are capable of true fear (awe) concerning the unlocked secrets already in existence. In this book, when we speak of God, we mean the *Author of Reality*, the Creator of the power of the universe, the Being behind "the impenetrable that really exists."

C. THE DISCOVERY OF GOD

O Lord, open our eyes that we may see and welcome all truth, whether shining from the annals of ancient revelations, or reaching us through the seers of our own time; for Thou hidest not Thy light from any generation of Thy children that yearn for Thee, and seek Thy guidance.

(Union Prayerbook, p. 34)

To experience God is to experience the mysterious. It is to come into contact with the Author of a reality so much beyond our comprehension that we stand in awe of it and call it "mysterious" (i.e., beyond our understanding). Samuel Morse experienced God when he discovered and mastered the principles making possible the telegraph. Morse worked for years trying to transmit a message across space. When finally, after much seeking and laboring Morse succeeded, he exclaimed, *"What hath God wrought?"*[2] Morse could have claimed that he had invented some new thing, but he knew that he had merely discovered and applied a law that had always existed. When Morse came to know this reality, he became more acutely aware of the great power of the Creator. In his discovery and in his labor, Morse came into knowing contact with but a small portion of "what really exists," and this small discovery made him tremble in awe and exclaim, "What hath God wrought?" For Samuel Morse, this grand moment of discovery was a prayerful moment. It was a God-contacting, God-experiencing moment. By his diligent labors, Morse had earned an insight into an aspect of God's greatness. This glimpse of but a single feature of God's universe, this view of the divine, had a humbling effect on Morse, and he experienced a profound sense of "adoration." He could say now with Job, "I have heard of Thee by the hearing of the ear, but, now, mine eye seeth Thee."[3]

The person who experiences this moment of awe, this awareness of immense power awaiting our use, this embracing of the infinite, finds that in this prayerful moment, "there is life and food for future years."[4] Some of us come to know God by searching out the secrets of the physical universe; others seek contact with God as the Spirit behind living nature. The poet wrote that in such searchings, "I have felt a presence that disturbs me with the joy of elevated thoughts; a sense sublime of something far more deeply interfused, whose dwelling is the light of the setting suns, and the round ocean and the living air, and the blue sky, and in the mind of man; a motion, and a spirit that impels all thinking things, all objects of all thought, and rolls through all things . . ."[5]

D. LIFE FULL OF BLESSINGS

Just as Einstein stood rapt in awe as he contemplated the order behind the physical universe, so Wordsworth, the poet, came to his prayerful moment and to these "elevated thoughts," by contemplating the order and complexity of nature. These prayerful experiences gave Wordsworth a strength and peace that enabled him to conquer many disappointments in the regular routine of his life. Of his prayerful experiences, Wordsworth wrote, ". . . she (nature) can so inform the mind that is within us, so impress with quietness and beauty, and so feed with lofty thoughts, that neither evil tongues, rash judgments, nor the sneers of selfish men, nor greetings where no kindness is, nor all the dreary intercourse of daily life, shall e'er prevail against us, or disturb our cheerful faith, that all which we behold is full of blessings."[6] For Wordsworth, contact with nature was a religious experience. There are many paths to an awareness of God, but any of them can "impress with quietness and beauty," feed us with "lofty thoughts," and so strengthen us that not "all the dreary intercourse of daily life shall e'er prevail against us or disturb our cheerful faith, that *all of which we behold is full of blessings!*" Similarly, Shakespeare spoke of nature as revealing the divine power. He wrote there are "tongues in trees, books in running brooks, sermons in stones, and good in everything."[7]

For Wordsworth and Shakespeare, nature mediated the divine presence. For Morse and Einstein, the laws of physics mirrored the power of God. To all of these men, their prayerful searching, their meditations, their feeling through, and acting through to the "mystery beyond" gave a sense of a life full of blessings. This is one of the higher awards of prayer. *Prayer is "reaching for God," reaching for the greater reality, the deeper life.* Through this kind of reaching, one can learn to live with a sense of personal relationship to the dynamic power that flows through all things, including one's self.

Sometimes, as in the case of Morse and Wordsworth, a particular moment may have such impact that we consider it a revelation. What is revealed is another phase of reality. In such a moment, we seem to see, suddenly and forcefully, "into the life of things," and we humbly acknowledge the power at the helm of the universe. We say, in effect, "There is a king!" Henceforward, our life is changed. It acquires heightened meaning, for we know we are a part of an infinite greatness. This moment of awareness, this prayerful moment, then nourishes our future years with the food of inspiration. Having once come forcefully into contact with such power and beauty, we can never again forget that it is there, and that we are a part of the same stream from which it flows.

III

What Is Man That God Should Be Concerned About Him?

"The Lord of the Universe is *our* Redeemer."
(*Union Prayerbook*, p. 31)

A. THE ANSWER OF ISRAEL

1. Man Is Made in the "Image of God."[1]

SOME WORSHIPERS ASK, "WHAT IS THE VALUE OF THE PRAYERS of adoration in the Prayer Service?" The function of these prayers is to make us aware that we belong to something infinitely greater than ourselves. They enable us to understand that we are not as small and as impotent as we sometimes think. God does not need our praise, but we need to remind ourselves of the power to which we are linked. There is a danger, however, in the mere adoration of God as the Author of Creation. Unless we continue to the next step in prayer, we may become convinced of our own insignificance and helplessness. Judaism does not doubt that the Creator of the Universe and man are intimately related. Each Sabbath we pray, "The Lord of the Universe is *our redeemer*." He who places the stars in their individual orbits is interested in us, too. We are not apart from His greatness.

The Psalmist has no problem in reconciling this seeming contradiction. He declares (Psalms 8:4-7) "When I behold Thy heavens, the work of Thy fingers, the moon and the stars, which Thou hast established; what is man, that Thou art mindful of him, and the son of man, that Thou thinkest of him? Yet, Thou hast made him but little lower than the angels, and hast crowned him with glory and honor. Thou hast made him to have dominion over the works of Thy hands . . ." How quickly this Psalm, which we use in our Prayer Service, passes from an adoration of God to a reminder that man is God's noblest creation. Indeed, he is appointed by God to share in the control of God's created things.

The rabbis of Eastern Europe, in the eighteenth century, taught, "The greatest evil is when you forget that you are the son of a king!"[2] This was their way of saying that man will live optimistically and creatively only if he remembers, at all times, that he is wonderfully formed by a God who cares. In our highly urbanized and competitive society, it is easy for the individual to conclude that he is an insignificant speck in a swarming mass. The pages of Genesis would teach us otherwise. The text informs us that man is made in the "image of God."[3] While contemporaries of the early Hebrews taught that the king was divine and that his subjects were a mere shadow of the king's being, the Hebrews taught that each man is made of the divine stuff itself!

Prayer is not possible unless one has a reasonable evaluation of his own importance. Those who belittle or hate themselves despair of ever leading meaningful lives and find it difficult to pray. To pray, you must believe yourself capable of change and growth towards the "image of the Divine." Looked at in this light, prayer is an exalted tool leading to the reawakening of the sense of one's own worthwhileness. It is a channel by which the individual river can link itself to the great ocean of life. It is a way of learning, a way of reaffirming the fact that we live in a kingdom greater than the kingdom of the individual. Prayer is a way to the tapping of a power greater than the individual believes he has. It is the process of becoming increasingly a part of the greater life in which we move and which flows through us at all times.

a. The Far-Near God, The God of Love

The truly religious person does not have great difficulty in bridging the gap between the universal God and the personal God. Judaism says simply, "God is far, and He is near. He is the far-near God."[4] Our Reform Prayer Book, p. 39, reads, "Thou art as close to us as breathing, and yet art farther than the farthermost star." The God of the heavens is the God of the heart. Two conclusions follow from this apparent contradiction. God is both the God of love and the God of laws.

(1) He Who Prays Goes in Search of Love—

"Great has been Thy love for us and Thy compassion boundless"—

(*Union Prayerbook*, p. 118)

19

Throughout the years, Jews have prayed in a specific way. The morning, afternoon, and evening services of the Jewish Prayer Book, which my teacher, Dr. Henry Slonimsky, has called "the greatest contribution of the Jews to the world," all begin with prayers extolling God as the Author of the vast creation.[5] Immediately thereafter, however, there is a prayer which teaches that God created the world because of his love for man.[6] The morning prayer reads:

> a-ha-vah ra-bah a-hav-ta-nu . . .
> With a great love hast Thou loved us . . .

This is the dimension that religion adds to the discoveries of science. It teaches that the creation was meaningless except as the evidence of God's love for His created things. In Judaism, God's love is understood as that which upholds the world. Love is the foundation without which the world would collapse. It is the spirit which holds all the material things together. It is the reasoning beyond the mathematical equations. It is the beginning, the means, and the end.

Small wonder, then, that immediately after this second prayer in each service expressing God's love, there follows the prayer, "And, thou shalt love the Lord, thy God, with all thy heart, with all thy soul, and with all thy might."[7] For Jews, prayer is, in essence, the process of learning how to receive, give, and use love. Prayer is a turning to the Source of Love, a receiving of the balm, and a way of learning how to pass on this love to others.

He who prays goes in search of love. He seeks a rapport with the Creator of the universe. He seeks an outlet for his complaints and a source of comfort. Prayer is a way of knowing, through a relationship of trust, what it may be impossible to demonstrate otherwise. The Bible tells us that Israel was bound to God with "cords of love."[8] The group or individual who stands in this relationship to God is able to say, "I am not isolated. I live a meaningful existence. I am wanted. I am bound together with the Heart of the universe and with the created things in it. We embrace each other. We serve and give to each other." Prayer is the way to a partnership with God in the continuing creation.

(2) Who Can Pray?

Only those can pray who are not afraid to love. The fear of trusting, the fear of giving, is a curse which plagues so many adults. Psychiatrists, like Erich Fromm, tell us that man's greatest fear is the fear of giving his love.[9] So many of us have given our love to parents and older brothers and sisters and have had that love, we think, rejected. Most of us can look back to crucial experiences where we were tricked, teased, or cruelly betrayed by those we thought we had a right to trust. The wound inflicted by a betrayal of trust, by a rejection after we have innocently given our love, is the most painful of all wounds. For some of us, it never heals. Many of our "intellectuals," completely alienated from God, militant atheists, are those who, once, as children, warmly gave their love to adults and, today, nourish their wounds. You can usually tell how badly this kind of person has suffered by measuring the degree of his militancy against God, for, to him, subconsciously, God is the parent who ought to have been loyal and loving, and was not.

The person who refuses even to try to pray is frequently a person who says, "I am not going to be fooled again. I am not going to give again and be rejected." These people come to rely completely on their own intelligence and, in some cases, become strong and contributing people, but their super-independence is a cover for their disappointment. They once were the supreme idealists, the supreme love-givers, who were rejected. For this sin of their parents, they will never forgive God! How unfortunate, for if you cannot trust, you cannot pray. If you cannot give your love, you cannot acknowledge the receipt of love. To deny the urge to love a human being is unnatural; to deny the urge to find a Friend behind the physical phenomena of our world is unnatural. Each man longs to feel that he is a part of a meaningful universe, that there is a plan at the heart of things, that he is a significant part of the plan, and that the Creator cares for him. *Each man longs to transcend his individual aloneness and to become part of something greater, in which there is companionship and union. The person who prays learns how to give and to receive, that is, how to be a real companion, how to join himself to other people and to the higher purposes of creation.*

b. Learning the Will-Law of God

It must be understood, however, that by "love, ahavah," the Hebrews did not mean Hollywood-type romantic love, nor did they mean the merely contemplative love as understood by the ascetic. The Scripture clearly teaches that a man had to demonstrate his love of God by doing justly and by showing mercy to God's creatures. The Prayer Book closely intertwines law and love. God showed his love by the establishment of mitzvot, and chukim, and mishpatim, all words for laws.[10] We are to exhibit our love for Him by following His will as revealed in these laws.[11] For Jews, "love" does not mean merely mystic union. It has to do with deeds received and deeds performed, although it includes something beyond this, of course.

Our Prayer Book reads (*Union Prayerbook*, p. 118), "Great has been Thy love for us and Thy compassion boundless. Our fathers put their trust in Thee, and *Thou didst teach them the law of life (chuke chaim)*. Be gracious also unto us that we may understand and fulfill the teachings of Thy word. *Enlighten our eyes in Thy law (B' toratechah) that we may cling unto Thy commandments (B'mitzvotechah)*. Unite our hearts to love and revere Thee . . ." We need go no farther to show how this modern translation of a most ancient prayer combines God's love for man and His laws on the one hand, with man's love for God and obedience to His laws on the other. The clear purpose of this prayer is to have the worshiper feel grateful for God's ordering of the physical and moral world and to solicit the worshiper's obedience to the Torah or moral law.

For Jews, the religious life is the law-true life, the Torah-oriented life. In Reform Judaism, we understand the "Torah" to be the laws of morality woven into the fabric of the world and partially revealed in our Scripture and sacred religious documents. Living the Torah-indicated life is, in a sense, living in communion with God. Such a life is a form of continuing prayer.

Consider, now, that dramatic moment when Moses arduously climbed the mountain to speak with God.[12] Our Bible does not record the mystic ecstasies experienced by Moses. Instead, it tells us that his communion resulted in the compilation of a group of laws which, in themselves, were living evidence of the reality of God. Moses proclaimed to the people that they could best relate to God by following these laws.[13]

While Moses was atop the mount, however, the mass of the people had urged upon the priests the making of an idol, a god that they could see and understand.[14] The people had no patience for the long process that Moses had undertaken with the elders. They wanted, not the work that goes with true worship, but, the emotional frills that are associated with primitive worship forms. We have here the elements of an enduring conflict in religion. There are those, usually the masses, who understand prayer in terms of the peripheral emotional elements of worship, and there are those, like Moses, who understand communion with God as addressing the invisible Author of the Laws of the Universe. Those who danced before the calf at the foot of the mountain were satisfied with the experience of the immediate release of emotion. Those who climbed the mountain in search of a deeper understanding of God understood worship as the continuing search for the will of God and the practice and teaching of His will-law.[15]

It is, perhaps, too easy to say that Moses was right and the people entirely wrong. It is fair to say, however, that Judaism has placed its major emphasis on worship as "searching for the 'voice' of God," as expressed through the law that undergirds the moral and physical universe. For us, worship and study are, therefore, closely related, when study is motivated by a search for the truths that will aid mankind. It is not by mere coincidence that the Synagogue has been called the "Bet Ha-midrash, The House of Study," as well as the "Bet Ha-t'filah, The House of Prayer." In Judaism, these two concepts, prayer and study, are inextricably intertwined.[16]

c. The Burning Bush—Personal Communion in a Given Context

Do Jews, then, eschew the emotional power in prayer? Of course not. We are mindful of the fact that the emotional quality of prayer can deepen its significance. On the other hand, we caution against the prayer that is emotionally unbridled and which is not oriented within a certain context. Certainly, Moses experienced the deepest kind of emotional response when he "saw" God through the image of the burning bush (Exodus 3:2ff). This was, for him, a profound moment of revelation. So dramatic was the confrontation, that, henceforth, the entire life of Moses was changed, channeled anew by this event. None the less, as intensely personal as that experience was, Moses interpreted the deity in terms of the traditional Hebrew context. His imagination did not carry him away. Scripture tells us that Moses knew that he was being addressed by "the God of

23

Abraham, the God of Isaac, and the God of Jacob" (Exodus 3:6). The experience was both unique to Moses and not unique. He met alone with God, but Moses understood that the result of this meeting had to be interpreted within certain limits. These limits were morally conditioned. The result of his moving emotional experience was that Moses realized that he could no longer live in isolation from his people. He had to surrender the safe but passive life in the oasis of Midian (Exodus 3:1). He had to return to Egypt to help his oppressed brethren (Exodus 3:10).

The incident of the burning bush is a dramatic representation of the Jewish understanding of prayer. Prayer cannot be a refuge for those who seek escape from responsibility. It cannot be merely an exercise in emotional release, although it can include that. It must ultimately induce the worshiper to action, in terms of his better self. It must lead to deeds which link the worshiper and his community. We could summarize the experience of Moses in this incident, as follows:

(1) Moses seems to experience a personal contact with the Divine, immediately and presently (Exodus 3:2).

(2) He becomes aware of God as the creative power (the flame) that gives continuously of itself and is never consumed (Exodus 3:2).

(3) The deity, personally conceived, is further identified as the historic God of the fathers. That is, His nature is not changed (Exodus 3:6). He is a God concerned with morality and freedom, a *God who cares* about the weak and the oppressed. The Text is explicit on this point. It reads (Exodus 3:7) "And the Lord said: I have surely *seen* the affliction of My people . . . and have *heard* their cry . . . for I *know* their pains. . . ."

(4) There is a task for the worshiper to perform which leads him to service in behalf of the community. God says (Exodus 3:10) "Come now, therefore, and I will send thee unto Pharaoh, that thou mayest bring forth My people . . . out of Egypt."

Those of us who wish to learn how to pray might use these limitations as the framework for our experience. We Jews believe that this kind of prayer is best learned in the Synagogue, where one is taught about the "God of Our Fathers," where one learns in detail about the historical personal experiences of our people, and where one is constantly reminded of the community tasks stressed by Judaism.

2. The Relationship of the Jewish Group to God

It is ever a problem for the "prayer" to find a way that will enable him to relate to God. Judaism has always pictured this relationship in certain specific contexts. Jews have related to God as Law-Giver, as the Author of History, and as Covenant Partner. We have spoken of the tradition of Moses, which is that the Torah, the law of God, mediates His presence to us, and we respond, we speak to Him, by way of obedience to this law.

a. God as the Author of History

Jews have long considered, also, that God speaks to man through the events of history. The Decalogue begins with an assertion that is no commandment at all: "I am the Lord thy God, who brought thee out of the land of Egypt, out of the house of bondage" (Exodus 20:2). For non-Jews, this is a general statement which may not seem to have much force. For Jews, this is the pillar on which the other commandments stand. It is a reminder to us of a saving experience when God and our people worked in close cooperation. It serves to bring to life in the present a worshipful moment in the past, when Israel communed with its God. The reminder of the Exodus from Egypt permeates every Jewish holiday and religious service. This was, for us, a dramatic period of God-discovery, and it has helped to sustain us for thousands of years, in spite of suffering and wandering. The Exodus has eternally etched on the Jewish soul the conviction that "There is One who helps to save. There is a Power that makes for freedom." The burning memory of our historically recorded relationship with God has helped to keep us alive. This memory is not a detached one. It is a recall of personal experience. It happened to *us! We* experienced the power of God!

Our Bible states that every Jew, including those yet to be born, stood at Sinai.[17] All Jews are bidden to make the revelation at Sinai a personal experience. Our prayer service today is deliberately conceived to prepare the worshiper to enter into and to make personal to himself the experience of his fathers. This is why so much of our prayer seems to be an historic lesson, a method of teaching, rather than of petition. This is a unique feature of Hebraic prayer. It joins the individual to the community of past, present, and future, and insists that this is one ongoing community.

In the Book of Deuteronomy (26:1ff), we are told that the individual who brings the "Bikurim" or "First Fruits" to the Temple, as required by law, must offer the fruits, and then worship. The worship begins with a recitation of the history of the experience of the Hebrew people with God. It goes, "A wandering Aramean was my father, and he went down into Egypt, and sojourned there, few in number; and he became there a nation, great, mighty, and populous. And the Egyptians dealt ill with us, and afflicted us, and laid upon us hard bondage. And we cried unto the Lord, the God of our fathers, and the Lord heard our voice, and saw our affliction, and our toil, and our oppression. And the Lord brought us forth out of Egypt with a mighty hand, and with an outstretched arm, and with great terribleness, and with signs, and with wonders. And He hath brought us into this place, and hath given us this land, a land flowing with milk and honey. And now, behold, I have brought the first of the fruit of the land, which thou, O Lord, hast given me."

Through this recitation, as an act of prayer, the individual is brought into the discovery-experiences of his fathers, and is reminded that, even if he personally has not experienced sudden or powerful revelations, his fathers did, and he is not separate from his fathers.

This recitative form of prayer, this recounting of old experiences, this linking of the individual to the past struggles of man for a life of meaning, is a regular feature of Jewish worship. It is the essence of the Seder Service in the home on Passover, where families recite the experience of the Exodus, and conclude, *"We were liberated from Egypt, not just our fathers."*[18] This kind of prayer does have profound inspirational value; does give strength to those who participate in the prayer; does help in making life meaningful; does give a sense of self-appreciation to the individual who finds that his personal worth is to be defined in terms of an exalted community effort which spans both past and future.

So much of our Synagogue prayer is in this spirit. Those who participate in our services in an understanding way are released from their sense of isolation and loneliness, and they are linked to the continuing history of an ancient people whose ultimate

26

goals are uplifting to the spirit. In Jewish prayer, the limited strength of the individual is bound to the strength of an enduring Israel and to the eternal God to whom Israel has always related.

b. Entering Into the Covenant-Relationship

There is still another way, Judaism teaches, in which Jews relate to God. Our Scripture informs us that Abraham, the founder of our faith, made a covenant, an agreement, with God.[19] At Sinai, all Jews, those present and those yet to be born, joined together in affirming this covenant.[20] Our responsibility, within the terms of this agreement, is to strive to make the world truly His kingdom.[21] To the extent that we fulfill our role within this covenant, we maintain a relationship with our God, we commune with Him. *Even the Jew who refuses, perforce, to participate in prayers of adoration or petition is not released from his obligation to learn his role in shaping the world towards the image of righteousness and peace.*[22]

Our religious tradition strongly binds together the notion of God as Creator and Israel as the teacher of righteousness to the nations. On the Sabbath morning after Sukot, we read in the worship cycle in the Synagogue the portion called "B'reshit," the first chapters of Genesis, telling us of the nature of the Creation.[23] On that Sabbath, we also are bidden by tradition to read the Haftarah from the Book of Isaiah, where the Jews are commanded by God to be an or l'goyim—"A Light Unto The Nations."[24] Just as God created the physical light of the universe, the sun and the moon, so Israel must be His mediator in bringing spiritual light to mankind, we are instructed. One of the special purposes of the prayer of a modern Jew must be to learn the ways in which he may fulfill his mission as a Jew, that he might share with God the continuing creative process of spreading light.

Let no one feel that Jews, because of their limited numbers, are unable to be a strong, positive force in this direction. As citizens of the United States of America, we can work most effectively towards democratically conceived goals. Jews, as individuals, can work within many existing organizations to strengthen their democratic fiber and to expand their horizons. There are not so many dedicated people in this, or any other country, that a few consecrated souls cannot have a profound

27

influence on its development. Let us not take our covenantal role lightly. Our prayer moments can be moments of consecration to further the more worthwhile causes of our community.

3. Personal Prayer, The Psalmist

As one reads the Psalms, one can detect the pattern of the context in which the Psalmist prayed. The Psalmist prepares for the more profound portion of his prayer by first releasing his fear, anger, and frustration. Having done this, he is then prepared to speak to God on a more exalted level.

Consider Psalm Seven, for example. The author first appeals that he be saved from his "pursuer . . . lest he tear my soul like a lion" (vs. 3). There follows a confession of sin (vss. 4–6), then a request that the Lord pour out His anger on the author's adversaries (vss. 7–8). With the fear and the anger released, the Psalmist proceeds to a less troubled level of expression. In verse nine, the Lord is addressed not as a protagonist as in the earlier verses, but as a neutral Judge of all, the standard by which all men, including the Psalmist, is to be judged. By praising God, the author reminds himself that God is the image of righteousness (vs. 12), who is the surety for the fact that evil men inevitably will bring down upon themselves the consequences of their deeds (vs. 17). The prayer ends in the spirit of thankfulness (vs. 18). The one who prays has once more been restored through the prayer process to the mood of contentment and happiness with life. Let us note how far the Psalmist has come in this one prayer. First, there is the hot release of feeling, "the free outpouring of the soul." Then, there is a return to the appropriate context of God as the source of righteousness for all men. Finally, the worshiper seems restored to a mood of security and tranquility. Is this not a major function of prayer? Small personal cravings lose their compulsive character as we pray, for prayer is not merely the release of one's innermost feelings. *It is also the ventilating of our thinking in terms of the eternal values of love and justice which one associates with God.* If the Psalmist in this prayer had not conceived of God in the traditional concept of Israel, he would have ended his prayer with his first appeal that his enemy be overwhelmed, but he knows better than this. He knows that God serves as the standard of righteousness for all men, and *the "prayer" tries to lift himself to this image. He tries to make himself over in the "image of God," in this sense.*

The Psalmist loses his overwhelming sense of frustration as he reminds himself that the power of God is ever present and is available to him, as well as to others. This is also the mood of Psalm Thirteen, which begins explosively, "How long, O Lord, wilt Thou forget me for ever?" (vs. 2), and concludes, "But as for me, in Thy mercy do I trust . . ." (vs. 6). In prayer we can lose our sense of personal loneliness and be reminded that we, too, can be the beneficiaries of the never-ending life which flows from God. In Psalm Twenty-two we can trace the change that comes over the Psalmist as he prays. The Psalm begins, "My God, my God, why hast Thou forsaken me? . . ." (vs. 2). Then, the Psalmist is reminded of the experiences of his fathers, and he says, "In Thee did our fathers trust; They trusted, and Thou didst deliver them" (vs. 5). The hopes of the worshiper are raised, but he is not sure that he is worthy of similar treatment. He prays regretfully, "But I am a worm, and no man" (vs. 7), and again, ". . . my heart is become like wax . . ." (vs. 15). The worshiper works through to a higher note of confidence, for he states, "For He hath not despised nor abhorred the lowliness of the poor; Neither hath He hid His face from him; But when he cried unto Him, He heard" (vs. 25). The Psalm ends with the extolling of God as the Ruler of all peoples (vss. 28–32). In this Psalm, we see the saving grace of prayer at work. The worshiper begins, despairing and helpless. He releases his fear that he is "forsaken." He reminds himself, however, that God, as Israel conceives Him, is a Friend to the poor and humble, that He forsakes no one. He also reviews the fact, in his prayer, that God helped his fathers. He concludes that God will hear his cry also. The movement from despair to hope is one of the functions of prayer.

In Psalm Twenty-three the Psalmist summarizes the mood of the confident worshiper. God is He who "restores the soul" (vs. 3), i.e., brings strength where weakness is, hope where despair lies. God is our guide in the straight paths of conduct (vs. 3); He is the assurance of goodness and mercy, even in the presence of death and trouble (vss. 4–6).

The authors of the Psalms do not think of man as a puppet on a string, as the passive recipient of God's power. Man, too, according to their view, must participate in his own renewal. *The presence of God is the assurance of a possibility.* We humans have to work together with the Divine to help save ourselves. We cannot do so, however, unless we believe that the possibility for change and growth is always with us. Through prayer, we heighten our belief in that possibility, and we bring ourselves to the point where we can work with God to save ourselves.

Psalm Twenty-two has special meaning for Jews, even today, and we refer especially to the words:

> "Eli Eli lamah azavtani
> My God, My God, why hast Thou forsaken me?"

According to the New Testament, Jesus on the cross repeated these words, originally uttered by the Psalmist.[25] The experience of the Jew through the centuries, teaches us that the deeply religious person does not ultimately seek victory or success. The Jew has continued to pray in spite of centuries of persecution and seeming defeat. Why has the Jew continued to find comfort in his relationship with God under these circumstances? One answer might be in the courageous prayer of an East European Jew, who exclaimed after a pogrom, "O Lord, we will be able to bear all of our suffering, if only we know that we suffer for Thy sake!"[26] *The primary goal of the prayer relationship is not the material well-being or success of the petitioner, but the feeling of support, understanding, and purpose. The function of prayer in time of crisis is to permit the somewhat battered soul to return to life's battles certain that, in spite of defeat in past battles, he is still a loved child of creation with strong support for future struggles and with a sympathetic ally.*

Those who are embittered by the buffeting of life might well look to the Jewish people as an example of courage that will not be denied. In spite of the insane destruction of six million European Jews by the Nazis during the last great war (one-third of the Jews in the world), the Jews have continued to believe in the essential promise of life, in the power for goodness that is God. They have not accepted suffering in a stoic way, saying, "What can we do?" Rather, have they worked to find happiness in creating the Sovereign State of Israel and elsewhere, insisting that God intends for all of his children, including the Jews, to find life meaningful. Where do the Jews get this determination to stand up, again and again, after such staggering blows dealt by hate-filled hearts? Apparently, the Jews have a training which is rare and a discipline which is unusual. The recurring optimism of the Jew is rooted in his understanding of God and in his confidence that God intends for man to live a life that is reasonably fruitful. This optimism, this demand on life, is an essential ingredient of the prayer-mood.

B. THE ANSWER OF LOGIC

"The Universe Is for Me, Also"

Judaism assumes that God and man can communicate. Some people, however, cannot accept this assumption because of certain intellectual or psychological blocks. Let us try to deal now with some of the reasoning behind their doubts.

Suppose there were only one person alive in the world . . . you! As you walked (or drove) around earth's gardens and picked its luscious fruits, as you drank of its refreshing waters, made clothes of its raw materials, built a home from the living trees, and gazed at its starry skies, you would have to conclude, *"All this is mine,* yet I did not create it. Someone made all this and intended it for me. How fortunate I am!" As you continued to live in the world and learned that it operated as a plan, that the sun arose every morning and set at eventide, that the seasons came and went with regularity, that tides rose and ebbed with rhythm, and that even your body followed pre-arranged laws, you would have to conclude that there was a Planner and that these laws were evidence of His existence. As you observed that these laws of regularity were always present, you would come to feel that the presence of these continuing realities was not disassociated from God. *As He continued to feed these laws with power to operate, so His presence would be felt by you.* You would, ultimately, also begin to realize that the world was not a watch wound up and abandoned by the watchmaker. You would understand that the world was constantly attended with care so that it would not wind down. You would sense the power which was constantly being piped into the world; you would "feel the pulse" of God. In such a situation, if you were the only person in the world, you would know that God cared about you, otherwise, why would He give you such an estate *without your having asked for it?* Since there would be no one else to taste of the fruit, you would inevitably conclude that the

31

fruit was created for you. Why? God cares for you. *The gift of this world, is the Divine way of speaking, "Here is an expression of My love."* If you lived alone in the world, it would not be difficult for you to decide that there was a personal relationship between an unseen Creator and yourself.

1. You Are the Center of the Universe—The Problem of Numbers

Suppose now that a second person was seen on the horizon? Would you, then, become angry at the Creator and say, "I thought you made this all for me. You don't love me!" This is what millions of adults actually say or think every day of their lives. We take the existence of other people as evidence of the fact that God is not concerned about us. We ask ourselves, "How is it possible for God to care for each of millions of people?" Surely, this doubt is a projection of our own limited understanding. Our own experience does not extend far beyond that of our immediate family, so we conclude that no one, not even God, could be intimately concerned with more than a few people. (We might grudgingly admit the members of our intimate family to share our God with us.) It is easy to see that this is a small, human-limited viewpoint. It is a confining of God's love-power to our own human limits of loving. The truth is that man is not in a position to know how far His understanding and love may extend. The very fact that the universe is so large may very well indicate that He has an infinite capacity for love and concern.

Proof that the Divine power and concern extends to things infinitely smaller than the human being is seen by an investigation of the atom. The same meticulous care used in developing the laws which govern the solar system has been used in developing the laws governing the atom. On one's fingertip there are so many electrons and protons that you and I, if we could see them, could not count them in our lifetime. Endlessly, the electron revolves around the atomic nucleus, even as the planets revolve around the sun, without a chance of a deviation in their relationship which would destroy their orderly system. *If the range of God's concern extends to matter so small in size as to be invisible in a microscope, how can you and I intelligently claim that we are too insignificant to be worthy of His concern?*

The Mishnah reads, "He who saves one soul is as if he had

32

saved the world."[27] The truth is that in each soul, in each person, there is a part of all the greatness that is found in the rest of the world. More than that, if each atom is regarded as a complete world (a completely ordered harmony, self-operating and independent, much like our solar system in miniature) *each person is a universe of worlds* (made up of many smaller self-operating units). Certainly, a universe (man equals a collection of worlds) cannot be regarded as unimportant!

There is a legend, which was popular in the Jewish communities of Eastern Europe, which teaches us of God's concern for little things. According to the legend, the "Angel of Death" called to take the life of the mother of five children. The mother knew that she had to heed the call, but she expressed the fear that her children would suffer. The Angel took the woman to the site of a large rock and rolled back the rock. "Do you see the worms which have survived under this rock?" the Angel said. "How much more concerned is the Holy One with your children than with these worms which have existed under this heavy rock?" (The legend is particularly applicable to the problems of reality, because it admits to the possibility that some tragedy does occur in human life. The mother's life is prematurely taken; but in spite of this tragedy, all is not lost. One setback does not disprove the existence of limitless possibilities for survival and well-being in our world "even under a heavy rock.") Even the worm under the rock has received and is receiving the benefits of life from the Giver of Life. Man is not so small as he permits himself to believe. He is a universe of worlds, containing many infinitely smaller systems within himself. More important, it is in man that most complex and most highly developed systems interconnect and flower into being. Mountains are large, but they cannot think. Planets endure millions of years, but they have no heartbeat. Stones endure endlessly, but they cannot give and receive love. You are not an insignificantly small part of the universe; *you are the nexus of the universe! The universe was created so that you might be achieved,* and so that you might grow ever upward. You cannot grow, however, unless you become conscious of your significance and mission. You cannot grow unless you pray, unless you reach upward towards God. You cannot live meaningfully unless you recognize that you can consciously link yourself to the growing and giving Spirit of the Universe.

What has the poet (Tennyson) said of the tiny flower?

> "Little flower . . .
> But if I could understand what you are
> Root and all and all in all
> I should know what God and man is."[28]

The infinite pipelines of the Creation are in the tiny flower, linking it to all of the resplendent creation. Man is the crossroads of both the spiritual and physical creation. How precious must he be! Indeed, according to the Psalmist, he is "little lower than God-Elohim" (Psalms 8:6).[29] He is fully worthy of speaking with God. Only speak, teaches Judaism, and He will hear! Seek Him, and you will find Him.

2. God Hears—The Problem of Communication

How, you ask? How does God hear? The biblical Hebrews seem to answer, "He hears. We do not need to know how."[30] Modern man seems hesitant to make this leap of faith. He will not jump across the narrow abyss that separates his heart from God's. He insists first on a steel bridge across the abyss with road markers and signs. Modern man must know, scientifically, before he will honor God with his prayers; but is there ever this kind of complete knowing, and aren't there other kinds of knowing which lead to a grasp of reality?[31]

We did not know half a century ago that the human voice could be transmitted by phone and radio around the world, yet we have discovered the principle that makes this possible (the principle has existed forever). We did not know 25 years ago that the human form could be transmitted by TV via Telstar around the world, yet we have discovered this principle that has existed since the original Creation. Man can now hear and see around the world and into outer space. Can God do less? The cells of our body communicate with each other, without benefit of ears, in a way man does not understand. We know that our cells do communicate, however, for the brain tells the arm to move precisely five inches, and it does exactly that. Without the internal communication of our cells, man could scarcely operate effectively. We can only assume this communication because we witness the results of the interaction of the various aspects of our physical being. If we cannot understand a system of communi-

cation within our physical being, we must maintain a certain humility about our ability to understand communication of a spiritual quality. The religious person assumes the reality of spiritual communication, because he is a witness to its results. The fact that God may "see" and "hear" in ways of which we are completely unaware is, at least, an open issue. His lack of ears and eyes, as humans define these terms, would not deprive Him of the ability to communicate any more than the human cell is restricted by the absence of these specific objects. God may, indeed, "hear" our prayers far better than we dare dream, for we think of God and man as two separate extremes, but God may be the ocean and we the river. Our waters may intermingle and our currents influence one another in ways that are beyond our limited comprehension.

3. Gratitude (B'rachah)—The Foundation of Prayer

> "Teach us to be satisfied with the gifts of Thy goodness and gratefully to rejoice in all Thy mercies" (*Union Prayerbook*, p. 22)

a. The Problem of Comparison

Another reason that we think God does not hear our prayers is that many people seem to fare better in life than we do, when we measure by a certain set of values. We feel neglected or rejected by God when we see that some people are richer than we; some people have better jobs; some are healthier. It is the comparisons which convince us that God is far away or does not care. This, again, is a childish way of judging. Children measure begrudgingly every gift of a parent to brother and sister. No matter how much each child may receive, he is convinced that brother or sister has been given more because each does not receive the same things or in equal measure. It does not matter to a child that he has received a quart of ice cream, if brother has received a cookie, and he has not. The injustice of the latter seems to cancel out all of the love and concern previously demonstrated the parent. We carry this childish thinking into adulthood. average American may be miserable because he knows of people whose homes are 60 feet long when his is only 4 The person earning $10,000 a year is upset because som friends are making $12,000. The lady who owns a w attractive persian lamb coat may envy the lady wh

35

mink coat. It is the comparisons which make us wonder if there is a Maintainer of the scales of justice.

The Tenth Commandment is "Thou shalt not covet" (Exodus 20:17). Our fathers knew that comparison leads to the shrinking of the soul, to a smothering of growth, to the stunting of happiness and well-being. We rarely compare our possessions with those who have less than we. We seldom say to ourselves, "I earn $10,000 a year. This is more than the earnings of four-fifths of American wage-earners. This is more than twice the income of all the residents of Europe, more than ten times the income of the residents of South America, more than fifty times the income of the residents of China and Africa." We rarely say, "Look how far up the comparative scale I am." On the contrary, we usually say, "But look at those who are ahead of me. This proves nobody cares about me!" How absurd! This is the thinking of the child who feels rejected completely because he does not seem to be first all the time! One can be the son of a king, with multiple possessions and privileges, even though the king has other children who are magnificently blessed.

b. Making the Gift "Yours"

We can accurately gauge the weight of our gifts as children of this world only if we do not compare what we have with the assets of others. Coveting contracts the soul. Gratitude expands the soul. Recognition of the countless gifts that one receives just by being born can lift the heart. *Gratitude is part of the foundation of prayer.* For this reason, one of the basic Jewish prayer forms is the "b'rachah" wherewith the Jew thanks (and praises) God for such gifts as the ability to see, hear, and think, for food (even so much as the size of an olive) or for the privilege of experiencing a joyous occasion (like the birth of a child, a wedding, or a Bar Mitzvah, or a holiday). The parents of my mother, reared in the European Orthodox tradition, taught her to say at least one traditional prayer on awakening each day, "mode ani . . . I give thanks to Thee, O Lord. . . ." The person who does not begin by saying, "Thanks, mode ani," cannot pray.

Consider the boy who dashes across the open field thrilled with the joy of being alive. The boy jumps as high as he can for no reason, except that he feels the impulse to experience his own physical power. By this act, the lad expresses his gratitude for the gift of life. Each grateful use of one of God's gifts is, in a real sense, a prayer. Prayer involves use, for in the usage of a

power, there is a recognition of the wonder of the gift. The boy flings his body against the soft breeze, even as he breathes deeply of the spring air. He seems to pray with the very motion of his body, with the fibre of his being. His leaping, his ecstasy, is his way of saying, "Thanks, O God, for all of this, and it's mine. You gave it to me. I know you gave it to me, because I am making it mine!"[32]

So we come to a basic point. *The prayer relationship involves the ability to appropriate and to make personal use of the divine gifts which are available to all who will claim them.* If one were alone in the world, one would not doubt that all the beauty and power around us was a personal gift. The original gifts of God to mankind are all still present and available for the appropriating. They exist in limitless dimension, if we know where to find them and how to appropriate them. *The process of prayer involves a becoming aware of the never-ending sources of supply, the learning of how to tap them.* It involves the acquiring of the ability to be grateful for the gifts that are given before the petition is expressed.

In order to make the world "yours," that is to say, yours also, you must feel a personal relationship with its Creator. You must be able to feel that you are a direct beneficiary and not just an incidental beneficiary of the creation. That is, you must be able to enjoy intimately what you have, and you must be able to say, "Thanks." Traditional Jews would say this means that you must consider life a "b'rachah, full of blessing," and you must be able to recite the "b'rachah"; you must be able to proclaim the prayer of gratitude in word and deed.

c. How Do We Ask for Gifts (Tachnun)?

Again and again when I spoke to people and asked them their understanding of prayer, they would answer, "Prayer is asking for something." This is true only in a special way. In the first place, petition is only one form of prayer. Secondly, the mature person does not petition so much by asking, "Give me," as by exclaiming, "I need," and asking, "How can I fill my need?" The answer to your prayer may be in your becoming aware of the gifts available all around you, and on your learning how to use and to be grateful for those gifts. Jews have always understood that prayer was firstly, "b'rachah" (praise or thanksgiving) and not merely "'tachnun" (petition). The Synagogue Prayer Service begins with many prayers of thanksgiving, and, only later in the Service do we find prayers of petition. The prayerful person has ultimately to feel with the Psalmist, "This is the day that the Lord hath made, let me be glad and rejoice in it" (Psalm 118:24). "This day," such as it is, with its imperfections and failures, is still a divinely given day, with an infinite choice of gifts. Our prayerbook teaches that within each day the entire range of creation is repeated. It says, "(God) renewest daily the work of creation," (M'chadesh b'chol yom tamid ma-ase v'reshit).[33] How wonderful it would be if we could recite this prayer and mean it! Think into what spirit you enter when you say and mean these words! To pray this prayer means that you are sensitive to the constant birth of things all around you, for just as great miracles took place at the first moment of creation, so now these miracles are taking place. How can one be overwhelmed with his personal problems when he is mindful of the constant creative stream being piped into the world, all around him and through him!

First, the prayerful person tries to become aware of the creative reality, the giving spirit, all around him. Then, he seeks to acquire what he needs to live a meaningful life. How does he do this? A child would say, "Mother, give me this, or give me that." An adult does not pray to God, "God, give me food; give me a good job." An adult is expected to act as an adult. He is expected to help himself. Imagine that a bowl of fruit were placed on a table. A child would ask, "May I have an apple?" and then he is expected to wait politely for a parent to give it to him. An adult is told by his host, "There is fruit on the table. Help yourself." The adult is expected to exercise his adult prerogative of appropriation. So God says to man, "The world is before you. Take what you need"; as, indeed, He says in Genesis to Adam and Eve.[34] The prayerful man only seeks to become aware of what is "before him." He seeks the understanding and courage to appropriate the things necessary to answer his legitimate needs. The adult "asking" takes the form of, "show me what I must do to meet my needs." *What the adult seeks in prayer is not a handout, but a plan for action.* He asks, "Where?" and "How?" He understands that after the prayer (or as part of the prayer-mood), there is a role for him to play before his needs will be fully met. He knows that the prayer is a prelude to work and the key to a fuller life.

IV

Becoming Aware of Reality

"Opening the Eyes"

Lord of the universe, we lift up our hearts to
Thee who made heaven and earth. The infinite
heavens and the quiet stars tell of Thine endless power. We turn from our daily toil, from
its difficulties and its conflicts, from its clamor
and its weariness, to meditate on the serene
calm of Thy presence which pervades all creation and hallows our life with the blessing of
. . . peace.

(Union Prayerbook, p. 10)

"No limits are set to the ascent of man, and the
loftiest precincts are open to all. In this, your
choice alone is supreme."

Nahman of Bratzlav (18–19 cent.)

A. "GOD IS IN THIS PLACE"—(Jacob's Dream)

THE BIBLE TELLS US THAT JACOB WAS TRAVELING TO HARAN, AND
en route, he spent the night sleeping on a stone.[1] As he slept, he
dreamed of a ladder "set up on the earth, and the top of it
reached to heaven; and behold the angels of God ascending and
descending on it." In his dream, Jacob seemed to hear God's
voice, and when he awoke, he said, "Surely, the Lord is in this
place; and I knew it not."[2] Then Jacob remarked, "How full of
awe is this place! This is none other than the house of God, and
this is the gate of heaven."[3]

*The prayerful person comes to understand that this place,
wherever he stands, is the house of God, the gate of Heaven.* He
becomes increasingly aware of the signs of divinity within him
and all around him. Like Jacob, the prayerful person becomes
aware that it is possible for him to climb towards heaven (grow

towards God) from where he stands, and that the angels ("messengers")[4] of God are those who ascend (i.e., start from earth) to the heavenly (spiritual) heights and bring back to earth the power needed to help mankind. Those who find prayer difficult are those who pray under the mistaken notion that God manifests Himself only through sudden miracles and that He is to be found only in some distant place. They do not share the sense of intimacy that Jacob felt. They are unable to say, "How full of awe is this place (where I am)!"

B. THE REALITY WITHIN

"Thou livest within our hearts, as Thou dost
pervade the world."

(*Union Prayerbook,* p. 39)

Prayer involves the process of becoming aware of the resources for change and growth that await our appropriation. Judaism suggests that the supply for these resources are both within us and around us. They are nearer than we think. There is a Hindu legend which makes the point that man does not find the source of his greater strength only because he keeps searching in far away places and not within himself. The legend goes as follows: "In the beginning all men were like the gods. Then, man sinned, and the chief god decided to remove man's head and to hide it (within the head is the mind and the way to power). A council of the gods was called. Where should the head be hid? One god said, "Hide it in the ground." Another god said, "Hide it in the ocean." Another said, "Hide it at the top of the mountain." "No," said the chief god, "man will dig deep into the earth to find it. He will climb the highest mountain, and he will search out the bottom of the seas, but, if we hide it in man himself, *man will never think to look for it within himself.*"[5]

The Hindus used the image of the "head" (the god-head). The Hasidic Jews spoke of the "sparks," the in-dwelling presence of God within man, which ever longs to return to God. These East European Jews of the 18th and 19th century taught that God placed a fragment of Himself in each human being. This spark of divinity within each individual yearns to be re-united with its Source. It is the divine spark within man, the

40

Hasidim taught, which reaches upward towards more of itself. This reaching, this yearning, is prayer. We learn from the Hasidim that prayer is not merely the best in man reaching towards "the highest wisdom and beauty" (to use Einstein's phrase),[6] *it is actually the divine reaching for the divine.*

The Hasidic teaching has greater force than the Hindu legend, for it suggests that the power hidden within man is not merely something that is to be found, it is something that also has its own surging to be found and to find. A teaching hypothesis can point the way to a reality which exists but which is beyond demonstration for the present. Religious Jews have testified to the substantial validity of the Hasidic hypothesis. There are many powers within man, many levels of consciousness, many levels of insight, many levels of courage which man does not suspect he has, but which are there within him, none the less. *It is the function of prayer to make us more conscious of the levels of power that already exist within us but which await our developing them and thus "calling them into being."* We suggest the image of a well without end. The more we drink from this well, the more there is to drink. It is a well which has its source in the "Source of Living Waters,"[7] which binds us to Him, and which flows similarly through all men, thus binding us to them.

The Bible speaks of the becoming aware of the existence of greater power in terms of "opening of the eyes." This is the ability to see things which exist all the time but are not visible to people who are insensitive and who are unaware of the limitless layers of the creative mystery. For example, when Sarah was without child, she gave her handmaiden, Hagar, to Abraham, as a wife, according to the ancient custom, in the hope that Hagar would bear Abraham a child that Sarah, as Hagar's mistress, could claim legally to be her own. Hagar bore Ishmael to Abraham. Later, Sarah gave birth to Isaac, and she was fearful that Ishmael might gain the precedence that she wanted for the son of her own body. Sarah found reason to send Hagar and Ishmael into the desert.[8] Hagar was desperate. She was alone in the desert with her infant son and soon found herself out of water. She prayed to God for assistance.[9] The answer to her prayer was that "God opened her eyes."[10] The text reads, "and she saw a well of water; and she went, and filled the bottle with water and gave the lad drink."

41

We are not led to believe by the biblical narrative that the well was suddenly created for Hagar. The well was there all the time, but Hagar did not see it. Through prayer, her vision and searching ability were sharpened, and she was able to see something she was unable to see before. Her eyes were "opened." She became more aware of reality. This was the answer to her prayer! Through prayer, Hagar gained the courage not to surrender and to continue her search for a solution to her problem. Prayer is a way of saying, "There must be a way out. Oh, God, show me that way!" When the verbal prayer is over, however, the person still has a role to play. He has to search for the "way out."

Similarly, the Bible tells of the time the King of Syria was determined to kill Elisha, the Prophet.[11] Elisha and his servant were completely surrounded by the Syrian army of horses and chariots, and the servant tremblingly spoke to his master, "Alas, my master! how shall we do?"[12] The Prophet replied, "Fear not, for they that are with us are more than they that are with them."[13] Then, Elisha prayed and said, "O Lord, I pray Thee, open his eyes, that he may see."[14] "And the Lord opened the eyes of the young man and he saw; and behold, the mountain was full of horses and chariots of fire round about Elisha."[15] The story (II Kings 6:15ff) clearly implies that the "chariots" defending Elisha were there all the time, and Elisha could see them all the time, but the servant could not. Nothing new was created for the servant to see. When his eyes were opened, he merely acquired a power that Elisha (a prayerful, reality-conscious person) had all the time. We are further told, as the story goes on, that no battle of chariots was ever joined. Indeed, the "chariots" on Elisha's side were not really chariots at all. The vision was a euphemism to demonstrate that there was also great power on Elisha's side. The enemies of Elisha were defeated, the narrative recounts, because they were smitten with "blindness" (vs. 18). Elisha and his servant were victorious in the battle that never took place because they had "open eyes," and their opponents were "blind," because they were not able to avail themselves of divinely-bestowed powers (available to all men).

Most of the people in the world who live narrow lives are "blind" in this sense. For them, the goals of life are the shallow objectives of material gain and personal success. These people operate with a ten per cent view of the meaning of the world and with ten per cent of the power within their reach. They have

42

no vision, and they do not tap the wellsprings of well-being that would permit them to be content in the absence of agitation and anxiety. Like Hagar, they wander aimlessly in the desert of life, but, unlike Hagar, they never learn to pray, and they never have their eyes opened. They never "see into the life of things." They only use the resources that are immediately visible to them. They live in a world of surface reality. They eat the skin of life, but not the fruit.

C. THE POWER TO GIVE (FORGIVE)

It is worth noting that Elisha and his servant were able to capture the entire Syrian army (because the latter were "blind"), and the army was led to the city of Samaria where the Hebrew King captured them without a struggle.[16] When the Hebrew King asked if he should kill the enemy, Elisha answered, "Set bread and water before them, that they may eat and drink and go to their master" (II Kings 6:22). The Syrians who had come to kill the Prophet were so overcome with this display of generosity and forgiveness that the marauding Syrians "came no more into the land of Israel" (II Kings 6:23). The person with "open eyes" learns how to forgive and to be generous, but only the person confident of his own sources of power can afford to be forgiving and love-giving. Elisha would teach us not to be over anxious and not to be so over concerned with what tomorrow may bring, for there exist forces within ourselves and in the world which will make it possible for us to receive our bread and board. This, certainly, is the meaning behind the story whereby one hundred men are fed with the contents of one small sack (II Kings 4:42ff). *The person who prays seeks the power of love and the ability to share, and where men share with each other, there is enough for all.*

This same point is made in a story from a Hasidic source.[17] A Rabbi stopped to invite a man who was walking on the road to enter his wagon. The man looked into the wagon and said to the famous Rabbi, "Rabbi, your wagon is already crowded. I would not want to overcrowd you." The Rabbi answered, "Let us love each other a little more, and we will have a feeling of spaciousness." This ability to love others is kin to the ability to share, and we do not wish to share unless we can feel the depths of our own power. An awareness of this depth comes to us as we

43

pray and as our eyes are opened to the infinite life coursing through us and being fed to us. We become more able to give of ourselves as we become aware that there is a love-spirit in the world, a spirit of infinite life and infinite creative power which is tied to us and is concerned with us.

When Samuel Morse discovered the law of transmitting messages through space, his eyes were "opened." When Oppenheimer saw the results of atomic fission, his eyes were "opened." When Thoreau watched the miracles of nature transpiring around him at Walden Pond, his eyes were "opened." When a medical student first learns the law whereby food is transformed into energy, flesh and blood, his "eyes are opened." When a person forgives another and sees the response of gratitude and love in another, his "eyes are opened." The opening of the eyes means contact with deeper reality, awareness of infinite power, seeing into the life of things, touching God. It was only when Job realized the folly of comparing his lot with the lot of others, and when he took stock of the innumerable miracles from which each human being benefits every day, that he was able to say, "I have heard of Thee by the hearing of the ear, but now mine eye seeth Thee . . ." (Job 42:5). What Job meant was that his knowledge of God had heretofore been a vicarious experience. He knew God only in terms of what other men told him about God, but now he had meditated and pondered, and searched his soul, and prayed, and he had found God for himself. He had had a personal contact with the divine power; he had "seen" Him. It was this personal contact which gave Job the sense of serenity which he had been seeking. His personal contact had come about through a growing awareness of the constant creative power always feeding into the world.

D. THE TIME OF CRISIS

I lift up mine eyes unto the mountains, whence cometh my help. My help cometh from the Lord, who made heaven and earth.

(*Union Prayerbook*, p. 36, Ps. 121:1, 2)

1. "Before They Call, I Will Answer"

The experience of Elisha and his servant should be helpful to us in a time of crisis. In such a time, many of us, unaccustomed to prayer, ignorant of its meaning and its process, and ignorant even of what we should expect to gain from it, will, none the less, attempt to pray. Only in crisis do many of us permit ourselves to express a feeling of dependency, and thus allow ourselves to tap additional resources other than those we employ in a routine way. Prayer is "the unembarrassed revelation of the soul . . . a free outpouring of the heart. . . ."[18] In most circumstances, the average person is as awkward about prayer as he is about dancing and singing. Who among us feels free to express his deepest joy or grief, hope or despair? Prayer is the "unembarrassed revelation of the soul" expressed to a sympathetic ear.

In a time of crisis, we are in much the same position as Elisha's servant who, when he saw the menacing Syrian armies, said, "Alas, master! how shall we do?" We recall that Elisha replied, "Fear not, for they that are with us are more than they that are with them." Elisha could say this confidently, for he was a man who prayed regularly; that is to say, he was a man who was regularly in contact with reality, who was sensitively aware of the miracles (laws) constantly operating within man and within the universe. The person who does not pray regularly, who is not regularly aware of the miracles (laws) of life all about us, would find the counsel of Elisha short of reassuring. The insensitive person would not know about "they that are with us."

In time of critical illness, you will notice that the doctor is always more calm than the patient, for he is a student of the miracles (laws) of the human body, and he is aware of "they that are with us." He is aware of the healing power that is built into the human organism. He is aware of the emergency resources of the human body in a time of illness. My doctor has frequently said to me, "In most cases, a doctor's function is simply to put the body into a condition where it is free to help itself." If each of us were students of the body, we would be less apprehensive when most illnesses occur, because we would know that "they that are with us are more than they that are with them." In this case, "them" (the enemy) is the disease. Time after time, I have seen patients go into the hospital for major surgery with much greater anxiety than the medical facts would warrant. This is perhaps inevitable since we cannot all have the knowledge of surgeons and an awareness of the body's healing powers which the doctors have. Yet, if we could be fully aware of the forces on our side, our anxiety would be dramatically lessened. *The function of prayer for the person seriously ill is to make him aware of the power constantly surging within him at all times which makes for his healing, a power that manifests the continuing Divine concern.*

Frequently, the uncontrolled fear of a patient greatly hinders recovery. Prayer is a way of freeing the body to help itself; i.e., to work unhindered towards its own cure, employing the miraculous powers that are God-given and already present. In time of illness, we might well pray, "Oh, Lord, I am afraid. Help me to be more confident that you have anticipated my need, and that your divine power is working within me already."[19] It is not necessary for God to create a new miracle to save the vast majority of the patients who are in hospitals. The "old" miracles, the constantly renewed miracles, the divinely bestowed powers currently at work in man, are enough to sustain most of us. We ought to be able to tune in to this knowledge, to "see" this reality, if we are to arrive at quiet confidence when we are ill.

2. "It Won't Help Me"

> I gave access to them that asked not for Me,
> I was at hand to them that sought Me not;
> I said: 'Behold me, behold me' . . .
>
> (Isaiah 65:1)

Of course, there are many people who feel, "I know of the healing power in the body and of the built-in miracles, but this will not work on me. I am different, I am more sick than the others. I am in greater trouble than they. They got well, but I will not." These are the people who, for some reason, feel rejected or unwanted by God. These are the people who have not made it possible for themselves to feel that "the universe is for me." This kind of person could feel, if he were alone in the world, that the miracles were meant for him; but since there are other people, he decides that the very existence of these other people means that he has been rejected. The "self-pitier" must come to understand that his attitude toward prayer and God is the result of many factors which have shaped his life up to the present. His feeling of estrangement is his own projection of his past experiences. One poetess has expressed her inner melancholy as transforming the world in its image:

> "Because I see these mountains they are brought
>   low;
> Because I drink these waters they are bitter;
> Because I tread these gray rocks they are
>   barren;
> Because I have found these islands they are
>   lost . . ."[20]

The world reflects our inner attitude, and those who can pray are the optimists. They believe that the evil in the world can be transformed. They believe that God is capable of infinite love and concern, and that His power courses through all of us at every moment. *The problem is not is He going to help us, but are we going to let Him help us?* Are we going to pretend that we live in a parched desert when we have a limitless well of life built-in within us? The question is not will we receive of God's gifts, but will we use the gifts God already has given us and is giving us?

Isaiah, the Prophet, reported that God had said, "Before they call, I will answer . . ."[21] God has anticipated the fact that the body will occasionally operate ineffectively, and He has provided it with unbelievable powers of renewal. This is His loving gift to us. For the sick person, prayer means the becoming aware of the miraculous powers for healing which are active within him at every moment. It means the opening of the eyes to the forces that "are with us" and the realization that these forces represent the loving, living contact with our Creator. The person who practices the "art of becoming aware," who prays regularly, will make a better patient in time of crisis than the person who never or seldom prays.

3. The "Knowledge of God"

The Prophet Isaiah speaks of the idealized future king of Israel, the Messiah, as one who is to be filled with the "spirit of knowledge and of the fear of the Lord" (Isaiah 11:2). Elsewhere we note that the prophets sought to fill men's hearts with the "knowledge of God." Isaiah equates this knowledge with the "fear of the Lord." Perhaps he meant exactly what Einstein

47

meant when he spoke of the awe that comes to one when he examines the vastness of the universe, and perhaps Isaiah meant what Oppenheimer meant when he said that fear was his first reaction when he first unlocked the secret of atomic power.[22] Fear of the Lord means, among other things, understanding the power and the depth of some of the laws of creation as established by God. *Thus, fear and understanding are opposite sides of the same coin.* It is only the connoisseur who fears that a precious antique may be broken. Only the reverent person, who understands at once the power and the fragility of some aspects of the universe, fears a violation of some of its laws. It is a knowledge which comes only to those who have harnessed a great power, and the understanding of this power makes them aware of the infinitely greater power that lies beyond them.

The reverence that comes from this kind of knowledge is a reverence for life and for created things. It is a reverence for the infinite fragility and power of one's own life. It is an awareness of the miraculous laws which make possible our existence and sustain us at every moment. The "knowledge of God" means "knowing (in part) what God knows." God knows, since He is the Author of our universe and Creator of the beings in it, that the human body will recover from most illnesses because of its divinely-set curative powers. When we become aware of this "knowledge," we become capable of calm in the midst of our illness. A friend of mine, who is a doctor, told me he once treated Einstein when the latter was ill in the hospital. The doctor said, "Einstein acted as if the body involved were another than his own. He acted as most people act when they request a plumber to repair the plumbing system in their home." Einstein knew a great deal about the human body, and he had confidence in the knowledge of the doctor and in the curative powers of the body. Because he had this great awe and appreciation of the working miracles within his own body, he was able to be calm about his illness. He was aware of the sustaining power within him. He was in a "prayer-state."

Prayer is a way of obtaining "the knowledge of God." It is a way of gaining the assurance that in our crisis, as in our daily routine, "Those that are with us are more than those that are against us." *It is a way of reminding ourselves that the Friend who is with us has given us weapons and tools which are equal to the task before us!*

Part of our "weapons and tools" are the assets of our physical being (no less significant than the aspects of our spiritual being). For most of the years of our life we accept the health of our body as something to which we are entitled. We are not even aware, for example, of the miracle of the heart's pumping. Let us suffer a heart attack, however, and we are shocked out of our complacency. Our silent trust suddenly dissipates. We begin counting the heartbeats, as if our failure to count would cause the heart to stop beating. Invariably, the heart patient is afraid to sleep in the night, because he fears the sudden collapse of his physical equipment. Doctors, however, assure us that in the vast majority of cases, the heart patient who makes it to the hospital has an excellent chance of complete recovery. Further, the patient would be much helped if he were able to share the confidence of the doctors. Prayer can be a useful aid in restoring the patient to confidence in the built-in miracles within himself.

The heart patient has to learn to "float" as the swimmer learns to conquer his fear of the water. When the instructor teaches the would-be swimmer, he first makes the student jump feet first into the deep end of the pool. The student learns that the body itself has a buoyancy (built-in) that helps it to float. If he now wishes to swim, the student has only to expend a little effort and to learn the proper movements. So the sick person has to learn anew that the universe itself will hold him up if he doesn't fight it. The heart patient has to regain the confidence that the heart which has beat billions of times without his aid will continue, very probably, to pump a billion more times of its own miraculous power. In a sense, the sick person has to learn "to float" in the world, to relax, and, in quiet confidence, to let the power within him go to work.

4. "Thou Art with Me"[23]

Prayer involves this kind of rapport with the world, this kind of confidence that the power of God is within us and all around us, providing a buoyancy and a motor power which will sustain us, if we but provide a little energy and direction. So the sick person could pray, "I am mindful, O Lord, of the unfathomable miracle of my body. I am mindful of Your power within me at all times. I am grateful for the gift of renewal, for the miracle of healing that You have given me. Your power is no less now than when I was created. Knowing that You are with me gives me the quiet confidence that I will be well." Surely, something like this is what the Psalmist had in mind when he prayed, "The Lord is my Shepherd, I shall not want . . . Yea, though I walk through the valley of the shadow of Death, I shall fear no evil, for *Thou art with me* . . ." (Psalm 23:1, 4).

Again, we say that one of the reasons people cease to believe in the efficacy of prayer is that they are constantly looking for God to send down new thunderbolts from Heaven. It was Elijah, the prophet, who tried to teach us that God is not so much in the thunderbolt (the spectacular event) as within us (the "still, small voice," I Kings 19:12). It was Elijah's successor, Elisha, who tried to teach us the importance of searching for God in the things we already have, rather than in running desperately to find new revelations. It was the Patriarch, Jacob, who discovered that "The Lord is in this place, and I knew it not" (Genesis 28:16). God is here, where you are. Open your eyes!

5. In a Time of Death

> And when we ask in our grief: Whence shall come our help and our comfort? then in the strength of faith let us answer with the Psalmist: My help cometh from God.
>
> (*Union Prayerbook*, p. 72)

There are a few times in life, however, when it seems that "our tools" are not adequate for the task we have to face. Such a situation comes when a person who is dear to us passes away. What, then, is the function of prayer? *Through prayer we strive to change only that which is changeable.* The Bible records a crisis in the life of King David whose son, child of Bath-sheba, was seriously ill. David prayed desperately that the boy's life be saved. He fasted, threw himself upon the ground and lay there day and night (II Samuel 12:15ff). Apparently, the boy was too ill for the prayer to be answered, and when he died, David's followers were startled to observe that the King spent almost no time in mourning and showed no trace of bitterness, but, instead, washed himself, dressed once again in his kingly garb, and began to assume the great tasks that lay before him in his role as monarch. When his friends voiced their wonder at the absence of mourning, David replied, in effect, I have done all I can do for him. I prayed while there was yet hope. I can do nothing more now (II Samuel 12:19ff).

David is clearly identified in our history as a prayerful man. Many of the Psalms are attributed to him. He believed in God in an intensely personal way. Perhaps for this reason, David believed (1) You try to change what you can; (2) You must accept what you cannot change; (3) In spite of your loss, you must go on to face the important tasks before you.

Judaism has always encouraged mourning as the evidence of a healthy response to the death of a loved one, but it has always fixed outer limits to the period of mourning and has stressed the need of the mourner to return to the arena of life. The tradition affixed a severe period of mourning at seven days; then a moderate period of thirty days; then the outer limit of formal mourning as approximately a year. The specific prayer usually recited during this period is the "Kaddish," a prayer which, basically, is life-affirming.[24] The prayer links the worshiper to the effort to establish God's kingdom on earth. Its theme, in brief, is "In spite of my loss I affirm the greatness of God and the meaningfulness of life."

In Europe, superstitious notions became associated with the Kaddish and diluted its more basic import. It originally was a prayer said by the m'turgamen, or interpreter in the Y'shivot, the Houses of Learning. It was also recited when the students had completed a chapter of learning and were about to undertake another. Later, it was read at the death of a great scholar, who, in a way, had come to the end of a "chapter" in his existence. Still later, the prayer was read for all those who had died. In Reform congregations today, the prayer has much of the force of its original meaning. It marks the end of a chapter in a human life, and it marks the beginning of a new chapter in the life of the survivor, a chapter which, according to the prayer, is God-oriented, pointed towards life's higher goals. In the strongest kind of way, then, the Kaddish prayer reminds the mourner that the dead are to serve only as an inspiration for serving life with greater zeal.

Some people have the tendency to cling morbidly to the memory of their departed, as if to say, "My whole life was wrapped up in him (her). There is nothing left for me." The Jewish answer is, "Your loss has been great, but you are not alone. God is with you, and His creative powers are with you.

All that is left is the world!" Unfortunately, we humans frequently invest all of our love in one or in a few people. When they are gone, we feel that our world has shrunk, that all the doors are closed to us. How blind we are! In this frame of mind, we can use the wisdom of this kind of prayer; "O Lord, show me where I can find a new outlet for my love. Show me where I can find someone new to love me. Show me where there are new doors to open and new causes to serve. Open my eyes to the opportunities around me!"

Since all human beings must eventually die, the continuing meaning of man's life lies in his tie to something that constantly endures and to which he has a personal tie. For the Jew, God, the source of infinite life, has been his enduring Friend. One Rabbi wrote after a particularly frightful pogrom in the European community, "Oh, God, we could not go on, if we did not know that You were with us, and that our suffering is meaningful in Your eyes."[25] In the midst of his mourning, the Jew has recited the daily prayer, "Every day He renews the deeds of the creation."[26] On Friday evening, the Jew has held up his Kiddush Cup and exclaimed, "We do this in memory of the Exodus from Egypt and in memory of the deeds of Creation."[27] It is as if the Jew has said each Sabbath, "We shall not despair, because we know that the 'Power that makes for freedom and creation' is with us at this very moment." Let the mourner learn something from the Jewish people. He has suffered only a temporary blow. He still has as his allies, God, and a world of infinite possibilities. He has to believe this, however, if he is to triumph over his despair; he has to be willing to "open his eyes" to see the reality that exists.

So many of us say, "I am angry at God. He let my son (wife, husband) die. I will not be happy. I will punish Him." This, we must admit, is somewhat like the child who says, "I am mad at Mommy, I won't eat supper. I'll get sick, then see how sorry she will be." Those who punish themselves in this way, block up the channels of prayer and the fuller life. He who prays goes out to meet a Friend with open heart and open hands. He who prays in sorrow confesses, "My heart is broken. Help me to heal it. I have no one to love. Help me to find such a one. I have no one to love me. Help me to find such a one." He who prays must not be ashamed to reveal a broken heart and must come to understand the numerous new possibilities for loving and giving that are all around him. When God seems not to hear our prayer, the problem is within us. It is we who block up the channels of communication with our own conflicts.[28]

In time of crisis, such as in a time of mourning, the one who prays has to feel there is someone (1) who is superior to the process of life and death, (2) who is concerned with his sorrow, (3) who will help him work towards a solution to his problem. Perhaps the solution comes best when we undertake a constructive task. Many parents who have lost a child stricken by a particular disease, say cerebral palsy, have found compensating love from hundreds of other children, similarly stricken, whom they have tried to help. Wives of husbands who have died of cancer, have become ardent workers for cancer organizations. Many people of means, who had hoarded their money before, suddenly decide to give freely to charity in the name of their dear departed. These constructive outlets fulfil the ancient Jewish teaching that the name (the memory) of the departed be "livrachah, for a blessing." The memory of a loved one can hang like a millstone around one's neck, bearing the mourner down. On the other hand, prayer can help you make the memory of the loved one "a blessing to the living." The death of a loved one need not be merely the closing of an important door to life. If we will actively try to redirect our energies, we will very possibly discover that there are many more doors to happiness than we ever dreamed. Prayer is useful in reawakening our desire to serve others. Even the death of a loved one can serve a constructive cause if it stimulates us to personal growth and to community-serving activity. Frequently, one discovers that he has leaned too heavily on a loved one, and only the latter's death impels the mourner to step forward to assume the reins he had hesitated to grasp. Sometimes, the mourner discovers that by giving more of himself to others, he solicits a return gift of gratitude and love, and so, the open wound in the mourner's heart begins to heal as new blood and new life rush to it.

Judaism requires that the mourner either attend the Synagogue during his period of mourning or hold services at home. Standing at the side of other mourners, the individual soon learns that he has fellow sufferers capable of understanding his pain. Reciting the prayers of thankfulness and praise, he is reminded of all the gifts God is continually giving him. Expressing

53

the prayers of petition, he gains release from his heartache. Proclaiming the prayers committing him to the covenant and task of Israel to fashion the world in the image of love and justice, he gains new purpose.

6. Intercessory Prayer

We should note here the problems brought to the fore by intercessory prayer, i.e., praying not for oneself, but for a third party. In the Bible we note two prime examples of intercessory prayer. In one case, Moses prayed for the healing of the leprous Miriam (Numbers 12:13). She was healed. In the other case, David prayed for the survival of his son (II Samuel 16–23). The prayer was of no avail. The child died. The Bible does not speak much of intercessory prayer, and the general attitude seems to be, "We will pray, but the matter is in God's hands, and He will do as He sees fit" (II Samuel 12:22, 23). In later times, Jews tended to use intercessory prayer more, although the Rabbis cautioned against vain prayer as an insult to God.

The whole area of intercessory prayer is most difficult. The tradition gives us two views on the subject. One is reflected in the dictum "He is a sinner who refuses to pray for his fellow" (B'rachot, 12B). The other view is expressed in the dictum "The prayer of a sick man for his own recovery avails more than the prayer of another" (B'reshit Rabbah, 53:19). Reform Jews assume that the purpose of prayer is to enable something to take place between God and the one who prays. It is an intensely personal matter. What is involved is a reaching on the part of the worshiper. It is his searching, his effort to become aware of a power which already exists and which is awaiting his acquisition, which makes of prayer a dynamic process. We understand the response to prayer not in terms of a puppet acted upon by the puppeteer, but in terms of a give and take between God and one of His children.

The person prayed for is not a part of this dynamic relationship unless he is present when the first person prays. If the third party (let us assume that he is ill) is present when the prayer in his behalf is made, it is possible to say that he is really a participant in the prayer, that he is affected by the prayer of the first person. He is affected because he knows that someone cares about him, and he becomes mindful of the fact that another person has hopes for him. When he is present, the third person can receive a transfusion of strength, of optimism, of will, when the first person prays hopefully. It might be said that the third person is a silent participant in the prayer of the first person, in such a situation.

When the third person is not physically present during the prayer, it would seem that he must, at least, know of the prayer in his behalf, if he is to be considered a part of the prayer situation.

When God acts upon a person, without a call having come from that person, or without the consciousness of that person, we have something other than an "answer" to prayer. Certainly, God is able to act upon us before we call. Our existence is witness to that fact. Our health, when we do not pray for health, is witness to that fact; but this situation does not partake of the nature of prayer. When we pray to God that He help a third party, that is prayer for us, and we can be affected by this prayer relationship. In this situation, the spiritual reservoirs of the one who prays can be enlarged. His ability to give, his devotion to others, can be increased. He can attain to a feeling of greater calm because he has expressed his fears and hopes to One who cares. What God then does in relation to the third party, who is not a knowing participant in the prayer, involves something other than prayer, for prayer is an act of knowing mutual participation.

We might summarize by saying that intercessory prayer has value 1) for the first person praying in behalf of another, and 2) it has value for the person prayed for, if he is present or knows of the prayer of intercession. Otherwise, we enter into a realm of which we have no knowledge, although it is evident that God acts upon individuals whether they themselves pray or not. God heals and helps without our petitions, and prayer is a way to our knowing that He is *already* helping.

It ought to be pointed out that the viewpoint emphasized here is not an exclusive view, and intercessory prayer in the traditional sense is still observed by many Jews.

V

Prayer as a Discipline

THE PROFOUND MEANING OF PRAYER CANNOT REALLY BE GRASPED unless one understands that prayer is a discipline which requires rehearsal at regular intervals. The rehearsal, however, cannot always be a "free-form" expression. Even the parachutists who fly "free as the birds" in the sky in our newly publicized sport do not leave the success of their mission to sheer chance. These men study the laws which relate to the support of body-weight by the air; they know exactly which body angles to assume; and their timing is precise. In short, while it seems that they simply jump into the air from a high altitude, the truth is that they follow well-studied guides. Judaism does not teach that prayer is a flight into fancy in search of a mystical communion, nor do we teach that prayer is a secretive art available only to a privileged few whom the hand of a far-away god has touched. For informed and sensitive Jews, prayer is a continuing work-relationship with our Creator in dealing with real problems. There are laws governing the prayer process, and we are bidden to master those laws. Those who speak of prayer, except in rare instances, as mystical contacts, are, we think, playing a game which could be dangerous.

There is in every man the impulse to pray, however dim it might seem to be. The involuntary surge, which seems to come to the fore in time of crisis, reflects a deeply ingrained need in man to reach out to his roots and reservoir. The wise person will try to understand this need and to channel it in the most constructive way by proper cultivation and exercise. For Jews, prayer is a process which begins with 1) thought and study, 2) continues through the stage of verbalization (the conversation with the Power that motivates us and attracts us may be either vocal or silent), and 3) continues through the action inspired by and ennobled by the prior steps.

On the opposite end of the spectrum from those who leap into space where prayer is concerned are those who do not feel that prayer is a vital issue. It is not a "felt need," to use the psychologist's phrase. Most people accept the existence of a god but do not consciously sense a personal relationship with him. They are not aware of the magnetic push and pull of which the Hasidim spoke. Many of us are religious only in a formal sense. We are in much the same position as Voltaire, the outspoken Frenchman of the eighteenth century. The story is told that Voltaire, who was noted for his sharp criticism of the popular concepts of religion, was once walking down the streets of Paris with a friend.[1] They happened to pass a religious functionary carrying an Ikon. Voltaire paused, assumed a military posture, and saluted. His friend, somewhat astonished, asked, "Why do you, the staunch critic of religion, pay your respects to God?" Voltaire replied, "God and I do not speak, but we salute!" Most of us do not maintain a regular speaking relationship with God. We prefer to be a member of the religious fraternity from a respectful distance. Judaism submits that there can be no real religiosity, unless one seeks to "speak" with God, unless one seeks a continuing relationship with the source of love and life. In spite of the difficulties of entering into this kind of relationship in a realistic manner, we hold that the person who wants to live life at its fullest, as a secure and loved person, will zealously search out his roots in the Divine.

A. THE IMITATION OF GOD

The goal of Judaism is to teach and to guide mankind to imitate God. We conceive of God as a just and merciful God, filled with love and forgiveness. Our Scripture teaches that He has commanded us, "Ye shall be holy because I, the Lord, your God, am holy."[2] To imitate the divine, men have to realize the divine potential within themselves. To ask, how does a man pray, is to ask how does a man seek to realize the divine potential within himself? How does he try to become God-like? How does he try to grow towards God? How does he seek to prepare himself to do God's work? Most people think of prayer merely in the formal sense of what a man does when he is in the synagogue or church, or they think of prayer merely in the sense of the words a man pointedly addresses to God. Prayer may be each of these things, but it involves a great many other things. *Prayer is a process which begins with thoughts, involves*

57

words and study, and, in a sense, includes the activity for which the thought, words, and study were the preparation. When this process is in continuous actualization, it might be called "the prayer-state," and a man could be in that state when he is thinking or studying or speaking or acting, but, most properly, when these activities merge into one another. We are not talking about something ethereal, then, when we speak of prayer. We are speaking of one step, which is part of many other interacting steps, leading towards a fuller and more meaningful life.

B. OUR GOD-IMAGE

Recently, a young school teacher told me, "When my father was very ill, I prayed for the first time in many years, and I felt uncomfortable. I didn't really know to whom I was praying." This young lady is typical of most Americans today. We pray only in acute crisis, and when we do attempt to pray, we are not even certain of the procedure. For most of us, prayer is an awkward and rare experience. Many intellectual people feel awkward at prayer because they are embarrassed that they have no precise definition of God. We, who are raised in a super-rationalistic-scientific atmosphere, call so little upon the knowledge of the heart, that we are embarrassed when, on rarest occasions, we yield to its demands. It could well be that, as the poet said, "the heart has a mind, the mind knows not of."

Maimonides taught that the moment we start defining what God is we approach idolatry. All great religious figures have understood that man's ability to comprehend the nature of God in His totality is so limited that once we start to say what we think God is, we are defining Him in human terms and in inadequate terms. Maimonides suggests that we are bound to define Him incorrectly because of our limited understanding. His view was that when we compose a definition of God, we set up an incorrect image, and in worshipping it, we commit idolatry. The greatest religious teachers, like Moses and Maimonides, have always suggested that we do not use an image for God, and that we do not attempt to define Him. Judaism has always taught that we can really know God only through what He does, by His deeds.[3] His created world, the existence of complex and precious human beings, the reality of love, justice and mercy, these are the evidences of divinity which we trace to their source, a Being beyond our comprehension.

1. Our Noblest Projection

Einstein suggested that no matter what we may learn about our universe, and no matter what may be the measure of our attainment towards "the highest wisdom and most radiant beauty," we will never understand God more than "primitively." In brief, we can gain insights into God's wisdom and power; we can see the beginning or the crystallization of things; but we can never confront God in His total being. Martin Buber, who has written much on this theme in modern times, assumes this much to be true. Nevertheless, he says, men do construct a God image, and "Our construction of a God image shows our greatness. . . . It is our noblest projection."[4] If we are honest with ourselves, we will admit that the image we have of God changes as we ourselves grow in stature, as we climb another rung on the ladder towards the highest wisdom. In a way, we could say our image of God is a measure of our own developed being, a reflection of the greatness towards which we are capable of reaching at that particular point of our life.

In the Book of Zohar, written in 13th century Spain, there are these words, ". . . *But, of a truth, the Holy one makes Himself known to every one according to the measure of his understanding and his capacity to attach himself to the spirit of divine wisdom; a full knowledge is beyond the reach of any being.*"[5] The "god" in which the agnostic or atheist does not believe, is frequently merely a god-concept which the person once had and has rejected. (The atheist chooses the god-concept in which he prefers not to believe.) The truly religious person must reject many god-concepts as he himself grows in stature, but he most assuredly does not reject God. The religious person understands that his current god-concept is a key which he uses to open one door in God's mansion. When he opens that door and gathers the new truth, the seeker of God must then fashion a new key which will open the next door and lead him to a greater truth, a step nearer to the reality of God. *None the less, each of these concepts has a kernel of truth which they share in common.* Each concept leading to the Divine has a reality-factor which is more true than the dimension of the particular concept. Each God-concept posits that:

59

a) There is Someone who cares (There is a King)
b) This Someone created the universe that it might be a blessing to man (I am His son, daughter)
c) Man can increase his blessings by approaching nearer to God, by acquiring a greater measure of the divine knowledge and power (I have a role to play)

This is what Buber meant when he said, *"A religious person senses a reality which is truer than any of his projections."*[6] Einstein said, *". . . this knowledge, this feeling, is at the center of true religiousness."*[7] The mathematician needs only three points to plot an entire circle. The seasoned sailor does not need to see land to know when it is looming in the distance. The person with a developed understanding of the universe has this same certain knowledge of a God, who, though imageless, nevertheless, leaves certain definite evidence of His power and presence. The person who really prays, feels that he is able to contact this power and to work with it to solve his real problems.

2. More Than a Concept

The prayer book speaks of "the God of Abraham, the God of Isaac, and the God of Jacob," as if to suggest that each of the Patriarchs had his own personal meeting with God, and each of them came to understand Him in a personal way.[8] *God ceases to be a philosophic definition only when we go to work with Him; when we attempt to imitate Him; when we attempt to grow towards Him.* Those people who belong to a continuing religious tradition, as we Jews, have the advantage of an historically developed concept of God which tells us of the results of concrete experiences of men down through the ages. By reliving our fathers' experiences, by working through the situations they worked through, we come to a greater understanding of God, but we must know that it is the God-work we do ourselves that gives us the clearest understanding of the reality of God.

The existence of God, however, is, of course, not dependent upon our definition of Him, but the image we have of Him may determine how we live our lives. Most human beings throughout the generations, have felt the reality of God, in spite of the fact that He was impenetrable. Different generations have interpreted God differently, and have, thus, served Him differently. It is not unfair to say that the understanding Western man has of God is the result of thousands of years of searching and struggling towards a higher truth.

C. GROWING TOWARDS GOD: The Beckoning God

Once a disciple said to a Hasidic Rabbi, "Master, why is it that God sometimes seems so far away?" The Rabbi replied, "Imagine a father teaching a child to walk. He does not hold on to the child. On the contrary, he holds his arms outstretched away from the child, and the child walks forward, in between the arms. As the child comes forward, the father moves further away. How else is the child to learn to walk?"[9] All is not a bed of roses for us on this earth, because were it otherwise, we would never develop into our humanity. We would never rise towards God. God is near with His outstretched arms, but He does not want us to remain infantile. He wants us to develop our divinity. And as we go forward (seemingly alone), we come closer to God. As we develop our faculties for independent thinking and loving and sharing, we approach reality in life; but each time we come forward, the "Father" recedes, the goal becomes higher as we ascend another rung, the vision of God grows in scope as we ascend the ladder of spirituality. Once we have God wrapped up in a nice pretty package-definition stuffed away in our pocket or in a bank vault, we may know that we have a false vision. A God, too well defined, who serves as a crutch at all times, who keeps us in the dependent infantile state, is no God at all, but a projection of a childish wish. A mature projection of God (and God is not dependent upon our projection of Him) will picture God in the image of a beckoning God who urges us to grow towards Him in love and understanding. This dramatic image of the Hasidic Rabbi teaches us that God beckons us onward in order that we might develop our potential powers. The Hasidim called this "redeeming oneself." As we walk forward, drawn by God, we become less dependent on Him; that is, we learn how to fend for ourselves in this world. *The person who prays seeks ways to become independent;* as he grows towards God, he becomes able to deal with life's problems without despairing and without becoming over-anxious or fearful. It was Jeremiah who prophesied the time when men would not have to teach one another about God because each man would have the knowledge of God in his heart. The man who goes in search of God regularly (who prays) becomes less dependent (i.e., fulfills his potential as a man) because he learns what God wants him to know. The developed man communes easily and regularly with God "in his heart" and is sensitive to the nearness of God. He lives and moves in the prayer-state.

Philo, the great Jewish philosopher, who lived in Egypt in the 1st century, wrote, *"He who flees from God, flees into himself."*[10] We can apply this insight here. If going towards God means the development of one's better self, then one "who flees from God" is he who regresses, i.e., he settles for what he is, he "flees *into* himself" (as he is—not what he might be). The prayer-mood is a conscious attempt to improve oneself by the contemplation of a greatness towards which one would like to grow. Thus, our pursuit (imitation) of God is, in a healthy way, a flight from oneself (i.e., from the stagnating self). Prayer is the search for one's higher self, one's real self.

D. FINDING GOD REVEALED IN NATURE

There are several ways to attain to the prayer-state and to fellowship with the divine. Not all of us are capable of the same approaches. By training and psychological background, some of us find one channel more suitable than another. Some of us search for the Great Mathematician who set the electrons whirling. Others sense the Motivating Spirit behind the drama of human history. Some few of us have paused to hear the "still small voice" echoing from within ourselves.[11] Almost all of us, however, are aware of the presence of God when we commune with nature. The Nineteenth Psalm is a prayer few humans cannot utter in complete sincerity:

> The heavens are telling the glory of God, and the
> firmament proclaims His handiwork.

While no one can comprehend nature in its infinite variety, one can sense the immeasurable creative force behind it by studying just one aspect of nature like the oak tree or the ant. Each facet of nature leads us to the unity behind all of them. Wherever we intensely peer, we are filled with awe and adoration, and we enter into fellowship with the Divine. We pray in subconscious thought, if not consciously and verbally. The religious

62

person is one who feels that the universal is reflected in the particular, and it is through contact with, and awareness of, the particular in depth that we come into contact with the universal.

Isaac, we are told, "went out to meditate in the field at the eventide."[12] The quietness and softness of the field was, to Isaac, a sign of the tranquility he could find by turning from the clamor of his daily routine to reflection upon purposes beyond his personal ambition. Job heard God speak from the "whirlwind" with the swirl of unfathomable creative power that "shut up the sea with doors" and commanded, "Thus far shalt thou come but no further."[13] Tennyson found the infinite power of the divine in the "tiny flower" which, to Wordsworth, gave "thoughts that lie too deep for tears." Shelley was awakened to a sense of intensified life by the miracle of the skylark singing. The poet asked the bird,

> Teach me half the gladness that thy brain doth know
> Such harmonious madness from my lips would flow
> The world would listen then as I am listening now.[14]

The range of nature is wide indeed, from the ferocious whirlwind to the soft, waving flower, and to all humans, it speaks of power and gladness, of life ever-flowing; "It speaks to us of Thee, Our God."[15]

The author of a recent *Time* magazine article on "Faith And The Scientist" (June 29, 1962) wrote, "In the postwar technological explosion, scientists have . . . discovered that the more they know, the more remains to be learned . . . They have come to show greater respect for the kind of questions that religion . . . asks. 'Most of the scientists I know,' says Boston University Theologian Edwin Booth, 'believe in the immanent principle of life in the organic universe. If they are religious, they call it God. If they are not religious, they have awe and reverence for this principle. But it isn't retired, nor is it personal. *It is greater than personal*—it is absolutely essential to the principle of life itself . . .'"

For all of us from poet to scientist, nature and the awesome scope of the physical universe, from solar system to atom, fills us with an awareness of the divine. For most of us, the contemplation of the beauties of our physical world brings us to the mood that is called prayer, wonder, adoration, gratefulness for the blessings that abound around us. The experiencing of this mood heightens our love for life. In this prayer-moment, there is no petitioning or asking, but there is an answer to an unexpressed need, to be at one with the heart of life. Our point here is that the person who peers most intently into the heart of things, the person who disciplines his study, will come to a greater awareness of his personal identification with the deepest realities of life.

E. STUDY AS WORSHIP: Finding God's Will In the Sacred Literature

> The law of the Lord is perfect, restoring the soul;
> the testimony of the Lord is sure, making wise the
> simple. The precepts of the Lord are right, re-
> joicing the heart . . .
>
> (Psalm 19:8–9 *Union Prayerbook*, p. 149)

The Prophet Ezekiel tells us in the biblical book that bears his name (Ch. 3:1–3) that he was bidden to eat the Scroll of God before he was able to proclaim the words of God. Judaism has had a long and enduring tradition that the religious person must first be a student; he must first "eat the Book." He must first study Torah (the vast religious literature). He must become familiar in detail with the struggle of his forebears to contact God. He must make the God-contacting experiences of his ancestors his own; then, he will be the more able to speak to God personally. Bachya ibn Pakuda, Jewish sage of the 11th century, wrote, "The study of the Torah is as tillage is to the soil —ploughing and clearing it."[16]

There have been some who have taught that prayer is like inserting an electric light bulb in a socket. The divine current, they say, is always there, and it is simply a matter of attaching the bulb (your spiritual self) to realize the potential of light. True, God is ever-present, states the Jewish tradition, but there must be a period of attunement and preparation before one can "plug in" to His power and feel its flow. Prayer, our tradition teaches, is not merely the result of electrical contact. It is not that easy. Bachya preferred the imagery of farming. The soil must first be tilled, he wrote. It must be ploughed and cleared before one can hope to harvest the crops. Seeds must be planted, the garden must be tended, and the hard labor of harvesting is only a promise for the future. God does not simply hand us the gift of new strength, Bachya taught. "The aid that comes from God is like the rain that waters the field." God helps with some essential ingredients. He supplies the earth and the rain. We must plough the field. We supply the work. "The study of Torah is as tillage is to the soil . . ." It is a preparatory step in the reaching towards God, in the gaining of the "knowledge of God." Was it not the Prophet Amos who said, "Prepare to meet thy God, O Israel," (Amos 4:12)? The Rabbis translated this to mean, you cannot meet God (i.e., pray) unless you prepare for the meeting. A good way to prepare is to study the record of other men who have striven to meet with Him and have succeeded. Such a preparation is the study of Torah.[17]

So related was Torah study to worship that some Rabbis called the study of Torah by the name "avodah," the word used expressly to indicate the service of the altar in ancient days.[18] Although the recitation of formal prayers became the required practice in Judaism three times a day at fixed times, there were some Rabbis who considered the interruption of study for the purpose of prayer as unseemly. For these Rabbis, study and its attendant discussion and thought provocation, was a superior form of contact with God (i.e., it was a prayer-form higher than that of the fixed prayer).

The Rabbis understood by "Torah," not only the first five books of the Bible which bear that collective name, but, also, the vast range of religious literature, including the Midrash, the Talmud Commentaries, etc. The Talmud included the developed law of the Jewish people and the commentaries of the Rabbi-Judges when specific cases were tried over the years. For the ancient Jews, "law" was religious and secular at once. That is, there was no distinction. Thus, to study the "law" meant that one studied not only the Bible (the written Torah) but also the developing Rabbinic law (the oral Torah). Through this process, one became familiar with countless details in the day-to-day struggle of the Jews to build a democratic society based on reasoned law which was rooted in the authority of the Bible. This kind of study had, in the last analysis, a practical purpose and application. It equipped the student to understand and apply the laws of the religiously oriented society in such a way as to express his concern for justice and compassion. Contact with the "word of God" in this way informed, as well as inspired, the student to "love thy neighbor as thyself." Since every detail of the copious record of law cases and commentaries was deemed by the Jews to be rooted in God's will, study of the Talmud became a way to understand and determine the will of God. Such study was the equivalent of saying, "Thy will be done," only the student went further to determine what that will was, so that it might be applied to society and to man. It can easily be seen that such highly consecrated study can partake of the nature of prayer. It is not, however, mystical or abstract prayer. It is prayer turned towards resolving the day-to-day problems of life. In a sense, those who study the laws of modern society with impassioned zeal, seeking to discover and create those laws which enhance humanity, may be deemed to be "praying." Such modern legalists cannot be considered to be praying, however, unless, like the Jews from biblical to modern times, they recognize that the rights of man are rooted in the divine will, and unless they work at their task in the full consciousness that contact with the exalted law is also a way to the divine. The Jews called this consecrated concentration "Kavanah." It is an essential ingredient of all prayers. A familiar dictum of the Rabbis was "In all Thy ways, acknowledge Him."[19] For the consecrated person, the most menial task can become an offering to the Divine.

The study of the law, even when it is apparently rooted in the will of God, as in the Talmud, can become a kind of barren intellectualism if those who study it are not constantly mindful of its derivation and its purpose. One of the ancient Rabbis, Ben Soma, taught, "Every day, when a man busies himself with the study of the Law, he should say to himself, 'It is as if this day I received it from Sinai' " (i.e., from God).[20] Rabbi Johanan taught, "Every man who comes to occupy himself with the Law should regard himself as if he were standing in fire" (i.e., the holy fire).[20] It is clear from these dicta that some Rabbis equated the study of the law with participating in the revelation at Sinai, with exhilarating personal contact with God. In this sense, and in this mood, the study of Torah is truly a prayerful experience. (Indeed, we could possibly extend this and say that the study of other highly motivated literature, properly approached with Kavanah, could instill a mood of reverence akin to prayer).

We are advised that the person who studies Torah prayerfully ". . . is made like a never-failing fountain, and like a river that flows on with ever-sustained vigor; he becomes modest, long-suffering, and forgiving of insults; and it magnifies and exalts him above all things."[21]

F. LEARNING FROM GREAT MEN: "Frontlets Between Thine Eyes"[22]

There is a second way in which the study of the Bible and its derivative books can be akin to prayer. In the study of the exploits and trials of great men, it is possible to be inspired to share their longing and their courage. We cannot all come to feel as intimately as Abraham, that God walks with us, but we can share his pain at leaving his father's house[23] and understand his desire to create a new kind of society in a new land (Genesis 12:1ff) like the founders of America. From the study of Abraham's experience and its consequences,[24] we can be inspired to act with similar courage in a situation where we have to choose to break with past ties that brought us pleasure. In making this kind of decision, confident in the rightfulness of what we are doing, we can feel with Abraham that God "walks" with us. If we can act with the awareness that our deeds further the cause of freedom and justice, our mood partakes of the nature of prayer.

Suppose that we are confronted by a situation where it seems clear that many righteous people are about to suffer for the errors of a devious few. A study of the biblical text where Abraham contends with God over the destruction of Sodom (Genesis 8:16ff), can inspire us to oppose a wrong decision that seems imminent. The biblical story teaches that God desires the intervention of the righteous in averting disaster. It teaches that we need not accept an obvious iniquity as the unavoidable will of God. The story encourages us to try to change anything that can be changed for the better and not to accept disaster stoically. If we can act as an intercessor for good in a current situation, remembering that God wishes to avoid the punishing of the righteous, our action to avert an iniquity partakes of the quality of prayer (i.e., we contact the divine).

My teacher, Dr. Henry Slonimsky, has written,

> And so in prayer we must turn to the great religious geniuses, the Isaiahs and Jeremiahs and Psalmists, and make our own the visions they have seen, the communion they have established, the messages they have brought back, the words they have spoken as having been spoken for us because truly spoken for all men. And by an act of sympathetic fervor, of loving contagion, to achieve their glow, and to fan the spark which is present in all of us at the fire which they have lighted.
>
> This does not mean that all the deepest prayers and all the best poetry and all the highest music have all already been written, and that there is an end to inspiration. The future is open, there is no limitation on the wonder of insight and creation. But we each of us in our time and place have to husband the resources available and to warm our hands at the fires already lighted.[25]

When the religious tradition is studied in such a way that the student identifies himself with the historical actor and is thereby moved to courageous action, study becomes a catalyst to that exchange of profound feeling which characterizes prayer. The person who notes that the heroes of our Bible understood themselves to be addressed by God might very well learn to say to himself, "Is God saying this to me also?" God said to Moses, "Free the slaves!"[26] He said to Amos, "All peoples are mine."[27] He said to Jonah, "Have mercy on the people of Nineveh."[28] Is God saying these things to modern men? We, in modern Judaism, teach an affirmative answer. *The voice of God speaks at all times.* The only question is whether we shall hear it. A person lost in a desert cries out for help. To whom does he call? *To anyone who will hear.* To all who will hear! God calls to all of us, but who among us is sensitive enough, who has the developed spiritual high frequency to hear and to answer like Abraham, "Here Am I," (Genesis 22:1)? God calls to all as he called to Isaiah, "Whom shall I send, and who will go for us?" The problem is that only few hear and answer like Isaiah, "Here am I; send me!" (Isaiah 6:8). The person who recognizes the divine call to serve mankind, the person who hears the call for help, and who places himself in the practical position to serve, enters, in this precise way, into a personal relationship with God, into a prayer-relationship of *Ahvodah*.

Great men pray in their own way. Rabbi Leo Baeck was the sainted Rabbi who worked in the concentration camps of Europe, even though he had the chance to flee. He spent long hours at night with the sick, and he wearied himself daily to uphold the courage of his compatriots. If you approached him at his work and asked him, "Rabbi, let us take time out to pray," I am certain that he would have answered, "I am praying now!" There are some rare souls, such as Baeck and Albert Schweitzer, whose lives are so continuously spent in noble thoughts and deeds that it might be said of them, "They live in a constant prayer-state."

We pray when we try to reach as high as we can in thought, word, and deed, and when we do so, we are reaching towards God. There is such a thing as a prayerful thought, a prayerful word, and a prayerful deed. For most people, the dedicated interlude of the thought-prayer becomes much diluted as we attempt to translate the thought into action. Our resolve to be kind and loving somehow becomes diffused, as we become involved in our daily routine. As we are buffeted around by others, we forget to practice mercy and forgiveness. The thought-prayer is rarely transmitted in its entire force and power to the deed itself.

Our Bible and Prayer Book ask us to carry the moral laws of God, our dedicated plan for action, "L'totafot ben encchah," as "frontlets between thine eyes," as constant reminders of what we are to do, as a guide for all our deeds, as a measuring rod for all our actions.[29] There are some few men, who are capable of almost continuously exalted thought, who carry the words of God as "frontlets between the eyes." These men are regularly in the "prayer-state." For them, there is little difference between the thought, the word, and the deed. For these men become Godlike in the sense that they do what they say and think on an exalted level. This kind of elevated character should be our goal. We should strive always to be "touching God," to think and act at the highest level of which we are capable.

Please note that those who are in the "prayer-state," where thought, word and deed merge, are not "out of this world." These are people who try to do God's work to meet their own real needs and the needs of their fellow men. These are people who are not afraid to reach down into the gutter to help the poor and the fallen, and they are not afraid to examine their own heart and to admit their weaknesses, even as they seek the vision and strength to improve themselves. The prayerful person is capable of reaching both high and low. He is both forgiving of human frailty and demanding that humans reach for their greater selves. It is perhaps easier for us to understand the man who acts in the prayer-state of dedicated action than it is to understand the man who simply prays in thought or word. The Talmud tells us that "a man's deeds must exceed his learning and thinking."[30] That is to say, the person who seeks learning merely for its own sake and lives in an ivory tower, detached from the needs of man, will soon be inwardly corrupted. All of us are familiar with thinkers who become so concerned with minute definitions that they soon philosophize everything into nothingness. We are not concerned with "out of this world" prayers, although there can be no doubt that a certain amount of meditation and thinking and studying are essential to self-improvement and to prayerful-action. In the end, we apply the pragmatic test. *We ask, how has the prayer of this person enabled him to be a more effective human being in the active solution of his real problems and in the solution of community problems?* Real prayer is not concerned with pie in the sky in the bye and bye. It is concerned with fitting a person for citizenship in his family and community. This is why we must look to the activist people who live and move in the "prayer-state" of dedicated action for a demonstration of what we are trying to achieve through prayer.

G. SEEKING THE REFLECTION OF THE DIVINE WITHIN OURSELVES; SPIRITUAL ACCOUNTING (Hechbon Ha-nefesh)

The ultimate purpose of Torah study is not merely to inform but to lead to the inner development of the individual. This is a primary viewpoint of Judaism. *The purpose of all learning and praying is the development of human beings who are able to relate together on the higher levels of love and understanding, who are able to construct and participate in the good society on*

70

this earth. In the end, what is sought is the transformation of the individual and society.

Bachya, writing on the purpose of meditation and study, contended, "My aim is rather to bring to light the root principles of our religion that are deeply fixed in the unsophisticated intellect —those pivot principles of our Torah which are *latent in our souls.* Once we rouse our minds to meditate on them, their truth becomes clear to us *inwardly* and their bright rays will even be manifest to us externally. The following is an apt analogy. An astrologer went to a friend's courtyard, and divined that it contained a hidden treasure. He searched for it, and found a mass of silver that had turned black and had lost its lustre because of the rust with which it had become encrusted. He took some of the metal, scoured it with salt and vinegar, washed and polished it, till it had recovered its original lustre, beauty and brightness. The owner then gave orders that the rest of the treasure should be similarly treated. I wish to do the same with the hidden treasures of the heart; namely, to bring them to light and to exhibit their shining excellence so that anyone who desires to draw near to God and cling to Him may do likewise."[31] According to Bachya, the ultimate purpose of study is to lead the student to inward reflection to discover his own hidden treasures. When study inspires this kind of reflection, it partakes of the nature of prayer, for it inspires us to reach for the divine within ourselves.

We must keep in mind, then, that where we seek the "hidden treasures" in Jewish lore, our ultimate purpose is to reveal the hidden treasures within ourselves. We are seeking to develop that within ourselves which is real but latent. To do this, we may have to work at scouring and washing and polishing, but it can be done, and must be done, if we are to attain to our higher potential.

The study of the search of other men for a life of meaning can help us pray in many ways. When we study the profound searchings of others, we clear our mind of cares and doubts which are most immediately pressing. We are drawn into the more heroic struggle for broader purposes. It is related of one reverential Jew that he used to pray in this way, "O my God, my grief for Thy sake (at not fulfilling my duty to Thee) has annulled all my other griefs, and my anxiety on this account has removed all other anxieties."[32] We are not speaking now of the desirability

71

of building up a strong God-oriented guilt. We speak of losing minor cares in the work for worthwhile causes. We speak of purposeful living. The person who focuses his attention on the more important problems in life finds that his concern for his daily successes and failures diminishes. This is one of the legitimate functions of prayer, the re-focusing of our sights.

Ancient Rabbis, like Bachya, understood that prayer was a means to self-development; it was a vehicle for increasing self-awareness and self-knowledge. He wrote, "The benefit of spiritual accounting (one of the types of prayer) . . . consists of the results which the soul develops when it has obtained a clear grasp of what has been set forth . . . There will be formed in you a new and strange supernal force of which previously you had had no knowledge as being among your forces . . . You will then obtain insight into great themes and see profound secrets because your soul will be pure and your faith will be strong . . . This will result from the power of that on which you fixed your gaze and the grandeur of the mystery that was revealed to you. . . ."[33] Clearly, Bachya regards the raising of one's sights to the highest of which one can conceive as helpful in expanding the powers of the self. The contemplation of the greater reality solicits the growth of the self as if by magnetism. We are not moved to noble deeds unless we first fix our gaze on one who performs with love and charity. Where is this object which attracts our admiration? The Jewish answer is that He is everywhere, even within!

Bachya urges his reader to imagine that he is standing on a certain spot, behind and around which there is a figure he cannot see. However, if he takes a plate of wrought iron and smooths it and polishes it, he will be able to use it as a mirror to see the secrets behind and around him. The steel plate, Bachya tells us, is the human soul. The polishing of the plate represents the training of the soul in the sciences (contemplative) and in moral instruction. The person able to use this polished mirror (i.e., trained soul) will see the figure behind and all around (i.e., God). Bachya strongly suggests that as we look into our own sensitized and trained soul, we are able to see the reflection of the divine. It is the inner searching that leads to awareness of the divine. For Bachya, prayer involves this kind of spiritual training and accounting. Of one who undertakes this discipline, he says, will Isaiah's prophecy (11:2) be true, "And the spirit

72

of the Lord shall rest upon him, the spirit of wisdom and understanding . . ." Bachya urges us to search for the hidden treasures within ourselves, and "you will behold the true forms (of things) with open eyes." Like Elisha, Bachya believed that the prayerful person was the reality-conscious person who saw the things that existed all the time but which were hidden from the view of the untrained and the insensitive. The reality of God is evidenced everywhere. One sure way to find Him is to look into your own soul. Study can be the preparatory step which leads to the spiritual reflection which is the stuff of prayer.

VI

Some Functions of Prayer

A. SPIRITUAL REGENERATION

BEFORE ONE CAN PRAY, HE MUST REALIZE, AS DID OUR FATHER, Jacob, that "The Gate of Heaven" is here, wherever one is. We must pray where we are, with what we have. You cannot pray while frantically running. The person who wishes to pray must find a quiet place to rest. When Rebekah first met Isaac, he was in the field, meditating, praying. The biblical text reads, "And Isaac went out to meditate in the field at the eventide . . ." (Genesis 24:63). No doubt, he went to get away from the burdens of his daily business, to separate himself, if but momentarily, from the small talk of friends and servants, to be alone with himself and with God (B'rachot 26b). All of us, especially in our modern, harried world, need these moments when we can walk away from our burdens and commune with the vastness of the universe. In such a situation, we can come to understand that all of the things we think to be of prime importance are really but ripples on the ocean of life. In moments like these, the soul is refreshed, and our perspective of life is enlarged. Comparable to the nature of this prayer-moment is the calm we feel when we gaze at the sea for a period of time. The huge expanse of the water, the regularity of its movements, the limitlessness of the vision, soon bring us "out of ourselves," and the calm of the sea, its power and stability, become part of us, and we become part of it. Gazing at a natural object like the sea, we can gain an insight into the calm and power of its Creator. As we think of the limitless power of our Creator, we are moved to "adoration," and in praising Him, we empty ourselves of our miseries and take part of His calm and power into ourselves.

Rabbi Louis Binstock tells the story of an English engineer who was sent to Africa to supervise a very important project. Laboriously, with the aid of natives he himself carefully trained, the engineer assembled his equipment at an inland site. Suddenly, he received a cable to return home with the valuable equipment immediately, so he organized the natives for a rapid march to the coast. After two weeks of forced marches, the men sat down and refused to move. The exasperated engineer asked their leader, "Why, after driving yourself for two weeks, do you now give up when we are almost there?" The leader answered, "My master, we will rest here awhile to give our souls a chance to catch up with our bodies."[1] Men can be so wearied by mental as well as physical strain that they lose all sense of perspective in life. The prayer-moment is the "spiritual break" that we take "to give our souls a chance to catch up with our bodies," when we "re-think" the problem of where we are going, how we are going, and why. The prayer-moment is the rest moment "in the field at the eventide," or on the shore of the sea of life. It is the moment when we lay down the burden of the daily routine to get out of our own troubles and to let the ocean of life flow through us. The prayer-moment is the moment of spiritual reinvigoration.

1. "A Window to Heaven"—New Horizons

We cannot pray while running. We must first rest to gather our physical and spiritual resources. Prayer requires a studied moment of concentration. "The early Hasidim waited one hour and, then, prayed in order to prepare (or concentrate) their hearts for the Father in Heaven" (B'rachot 30b: cf. B'rachot 32b). As we rest and calm sets in, we attempt to set our sights on life's broader meaning. We attempt to see beyond ourselves to the next step on the ladder of life which we must climb as we grow towards the beckoning God. It is not necessary for us to encompass the total meaning of life; it is only important, for the moment, that we get a vision of the direction in which we must work and develop as the next phase of a continuing program and a continuing work-relationship with God.

Rabbi Abba Hillel Silver has told the story of a man who lived with his family in a village ringed by mountains. So far as anyone in the village knew, no human being had ever travelled beyond the mountains. For the villagers, the mountains were the end of the world. When the time came for the man to die, he called his sons to him and made a pact with them. He asked each of his sons to make an assault upon the mountain. The son who brought back the most precious gift would receive the greater portion of the father's fortune. The first son climbed as high as any man had ever been known before to climb, and he came running back to his father after several days with a rare fruit, proof that he had climbed to rare heights. The father was proud and blessed his son. The second son climbed even higher, and brought back a berry from a tree no one had ever seen before. The father was thrilled, and blessed him warmly, but worried about the third son. Nothing had been heard from him for too long a time. Finally, after several more days, the third son returned, exhausted, but exhilarated. "And what have you brought us, my son?" asked the dying father. The third son replied, "I return empty-handed, father, for I climbed to the top of the mountain where nothing grows, but, oh, my father, I saw the mighty ocean on the other side of the mountain!"[2] The story strongly makes the point that the reward for the hardest effort is frequently only a broader vision of a greatness beyond. The third son had returned empty-handed with no gifts for his father, but he alone had learned that the valley, which the villagers thought was the totality of the world, was just the beginning of things. As with this industrious son, so with the industrious "prayer." Properly, one does not pray for material gifts. One prays for a greater vision, for the lifting of purpose, for the increasing of strength, for the spiritual means of conquering the tasks ahead.

Small wonder that the Baal Shem Tov taught, "Let your prayer be a window to heaven." A prayer should be a way of enlarging one's understanding of the possibilities for growth and change. It is a way of looking out from where one is to where it is possible for one to go. *Our prayer is a movement of our spirit (heart and mind) from where it is now to where it longs to be; it is a movement towards the highest of which we can conceive, towards God.* The defeated person is the one who thinks that he cannot muster enough resources to master the problem he fancies to have overwhelmed him. The prayerful person (the opposite of the defeated person) will commune with his heart, with his better self, attempting to get close to God, and he will come to understand that there are more resources within him, more energy and determination and patience lying dormant within him and being fed to him, than he had ever imagined. He will come to realize that the seemingly overwhelming problem confronting him is really not so large that it cannot yield to work and patience. How does the Hebrew dictum go? "Chazak,

chazak, v'nitchazek"; "Be strong, be strong, and let us strengthen one another."[3] Frequently, through prayer, our vision is so enlarged that we come to understand that our problem has seemed to be great only because we have built up the problem in our own mind. A perfect illustration of this is in the biblical account of the two spying expeditions into the land of Canaan. The first was ordered by Moses, and the Hebrew spies reported, "We are not able to go up against the people, for they are stronger than we" (Numbers 13:31). The slaves who had fled from Egypt, accordingly, did not assemble the courage to invade Canaan. Joshua ordered the second spy expedition into Canaan a generation later. The second group of spies, children of the slaves, children born in freedom, reported, ". . . all the inhabitants of the land do melt away before us" (Joshua 2:24). Had the refugees from Egypt been able to assemble more courage, they would not have had to wander in the wilderness so long. So we, through lack of courage, wander in the wilderness of doubt and fear, when through communion with the "power that makes for freedom," we could arouse ourselves to heroic deeds. *Only those who want to climb up the ladder, who want to conquer fear, will pray,* and they will pray not that the enemy vanish into nothingness, for that is impossible, but that their vision be broadened, that their eyes be opened to see the resources available to them for the battle of life.

2. "The Prayer of Maimonides"—The Heightening of Purpose

A magnificent example of a prayer, in which the person seeks the way to self-improvement, is found in the so-called "Prayer of Maimonides." This prayer is attributed to the famous Jew who was the chief physician to the Spanish court towards the close of the 11th century. It is still quoted by many doctors today. One version is rendered as follows:

> The eternal Providence has appointed me to watch over the life and health of Thy creatures. May the love for my art actuate me at all times; may neither avarice nor miserliness, nor thirst for glory or for a great reputation engage my mind; for the enemies of truth and philanthropy could easily deceive me and make me forgetful of my lofty aim of

doing good to Thy children. May I never see in the patient anything but a fellow creature in pain. . . . Grant me strength, time, and opportunity always to correct what I have acquired, always to extend its domain; for knowledge is immense and the spirit of man can extend infinitely to enrich itself daily with new requirements. Today he could discover his errors of yesterday and tomorrow he may obtain a new light on what he thinks himself sure of today. Oh, God, Thou hast appointed me to watch over the life and death of Thy creatures; here am I ready for my vocation, and now I turn unto my calling.[4]

How much contrast is there between this prayer and the petition of those unlearned in prayer who vainly ask God for material gifts! Let us look more closely at the words of Maimonides. First, he acknowledges the fact that his vocation is one of service to mankind. He prays, "Thy eternal Providence has appointed me to watch over the life and health of Thy creatures." Immediately, Maimonides sets the tone of his prayer as one which is not merely self-seeking. He reflects upon his role in life, his covenant with the divine! Then, he prays that he be able to free himself from using his high calling merely for financial gain or for the exaltation of his reputation. He prays, "May the love of my art actuate me at all times; may neither avarice nor miserliness, nor thirst for glory or for a great reputation engage my mind; for the enemies of truth and philanthropy could easily deceive me and make me forgetful of my lofty aim of doing good to Thy children." In other words, Maimonides uses this prayer-moment to sharpen his devotion to the cause he serves. The next thought in his prayer is something wealth-seeking professional men might well bear in mind. Maimonides goes on to pray, "May I never see in the patient anything but a fellow creature in pain." Too many of the professionally trained people in our society look upon their clients as objects to be milked financially, rather than as persons to be helped.

3. Self-Improvement

Maimonides, then, begins what might be considered a second section of his prayer. This section has to do with self-improvement. He prays, "Give me strength, time, and opportunity always to correct what I have acquired, always to extend its domain, for knowledge is immense and the spirit of man can extend infinitely to enrich itself daily with new requirements. Today, he could discover his errors of yesterday, and tomorrow, he may obtain a new light on what he thinks himself sure of today." Let us note the verbs that Maimonides uses. He asks for strength to *correct,* to *extend,* to *enrich* his mind and spirit. This is the language of a man who seeks daily to climb yet another rung on the ladder which leads to heaven. This is the most exalted form of prayer, for in it, the man is revealed, not as a child seeking hand-outs, but as one mindful of the divine potential within himself which enables him to grow in power and knowledge constantly.

Finally, having purified his thoughts and having fixed his purpose at the highest possible level, Maimonides turns to his task and prays, "Oh, God, Thou hast appointed me to watch over the life and death of Thy creatures; here am I ready for my vocation, and now I turn unto my calling." How pointed are the words, "And now I turn unto my calling." It is a way of saying, "Now that I have strengthened my aims, I shall work to the utmost of my capacity." *This is a primary purpose of prayer at the highest level. Prayer should enable us to turn to our tasks with greater enthusiasm and ability.*

B. PRAYER AND YOUR WORK

May we so labor in Thy service that our lives become a hymn of praise unto Thee.

(*Union Prayerbook,* p. 29)

It might seem to some that the prayer of Maimonides is practical only for those who deal in dedicated callings like medicine and teaching, but the truth is that there are many more vocations where the practitioner has the responsibility to act as if his activities were God-appointed or oriented. The lawyer upholds the law, the policeman protects our lives. If the law has declined as a "calling" and has become just another business where the buyer must beware of the charlatan, it is because the lawyers, as a group, have not interpreted their position as defenders of the rights of the individual. That is to say, too many lawyers have not taken advantage of possible prayer moments, like Maimonides, to say something like, "May I never see in the client anything but a fellow creature in need of help." We do not mean to single out the law as an isolated example of a vocation that seems to have declined from the status of an ethical profession. Medicine and teaching seem also to have taken on the character of a business. Still, this does not mean that business must be conducted in an atmosphere alien from reverent devotion to justice and concern for people. Whether one sells shoes, dresses, or rags, whether one labors as a mechanic or as a clerk-typist, one deals with people, and reverence for people can be manifested in any trade and by anyone at any level in that trade.

One cannot pray unless he understands that he is made in the image of God. That is to say, he must be convinced that he is capable of infinite worth, and growth. Similarly, one cannot pray fully unless he understands that other men are made in this image, unless he understands that he can contact God through reverence for other people. The divine waters flow through all human beings, and the prayerful person becomes aware of the presence of God within the love-giving, courageous human. The person who is aware of God in the world sees the religious experience as a triangular affair, like so:

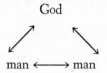

The divine spirit flows between God and man and between man and man. Even as two humans embrace the best in each other, they embrace the divine.

1. The Moment of Decision

In our society, however, the doctrine of "caveat emptor," "let the buyer beware," seems to be dominant in the business sphere. The person who is unaware of, or contemptuous of, the worth of his fellow human beings cannot appreciate his own personal worth enough to pray properly. *Respect for human beings, for God's handiwork, is a condition precedent to prayer.* You cannot deceive customers and take advantage of their ignorance all day, and, then, pretend to pray to the God of humanity when you come home. We must admit that the jungle aspects of our business economy mitigate against the prayer-mood and make the true religious experience extremely difficult. It could well be that we must make some serious reforms in our economy before we can hope to educate people to pray honestly.

People who hold so-called "second-line" jobs, sometimes feel that they are not in a position to bring the prayer-mood into their work. The mechanic, for example, will say, "I can see how the doctor can serve mankind, but how can I deal religiously in my work?" What the mechanic does affects people indirectly, if not directly. First of all, he may be involved in giving an appraisal on the price of a specific repair job. Since his is a secretive art, unknown to most laymen, the mechanic is in a position to deceive readily, or if he has respect for the customer, he can give an honest appraisal. In this way, the mechanic's sensitivity to human dignity is tested. Further, it is possible for the mechanic to do a make-shift or a thorough job in his repair. He can work at a minimum and put the car into operation on a marginal basis, or he can correct the fundamental problems in the car. The character and quality of his work can reveal the mechanic's self-respect and concern for others. It is clearly possible for the mechanic to bring high purpose to his menial task, but he cannot develop this purpose unless he spends time at regular intervals in meditation and in prayer concerning the direction he is to take in his work. *The prayer-area is frequently the decision-area.* The prayer-moment is frequently the moment, when in consultation with one's better self and with a "more of the same," i.e., with God, one decides to take steps that are decent and honest.

2. Working with Purpose

No matter how simple or menial your job, it can be done with a sense of high purpose. Contrariwise, those who are in high places, in spite of their opportunity for service, can degrade their vocation. This is the point of the well-known story about the reporter who came upon a group of workmen building a synagogue. The reporter first approached a bricklayer and asked, "What are you doing?" The bricklayer replied, "I am plastering bricks together." The reporter then approached the foreman who was supervising a group of workmen handling steel beams.

"What is your task?" the reporter queried. The foreman answered, "We take these beams and make them secure enough to support the rest of the building." In such manner the reporter went around to each workman and continually received replies only in a technical sense. Finally, the reporter came to an unskilled laborer who was stirring the cement in its trough. Round and round the laborer stirred the cement, a task which required much patience. "Tell me," said the reporter, "what are you doing?" The squat little man quickly replied, "I'm building a house of God!" and with obvious pleasure, he continued his stirring.

Whether or not we come home from our labor bored or frustrated may depend on the sense of purpose that we bring to our work, whatever its status may be. The prayerful person understands that what he does, however simple, will effect the lives of other human beings. He understands that he is a part of a larger and meaningful whole. The person unable to pray sees himself and his work as isolated. He lives in a blind alley. Through prayer, we try to link our lives to the broader life of the community. Like Maimonides, we can all pray in our own particular way, "May I never see in the customer anything but a fellow creature whose needs I can help satisfy." When this viewpoint becomes inconsistent with the possibility of "making a living," then we need to recast the mould of our economy. If we cannot bring the prayer mood (the reverent sensitivity to people) to our business, we are incapable of real religious expression.

C. MEETING GOD THROUGH MEETING MAN

1. Uniting the Divine Sparks

> O may all, created in Thine image, recognize
> that they are brethren, so that, one in spirit
> and one in fellowship, they may be forever
> united before Thee.
>
> (*Union Prayerbook*, p. 71)

We have spoken of the Hasidic Jews of 18th and 19th century Eastern Europe who taught that each person has a divine spark within him which longed to be reunited with its divine source. Prayer, they taught, is the reaching of the divine within man for more of itself. To the Hasidim, there were two ways for the individual divine spark to gather unto itself more of the divine nature. It could reach upward toward its Fountainhead (pray), or it could bind itself to other sparks to be found in other human beings and in other forms of existence. This, too, was a kind of prayer. In a broad sense, then, for the Hasidim, when one man bound himself to another man, he was gathering more of the divine unto himself. To love one's comrade was to participate in a uniting of otherwise isolated divine sparks. Love between people was an effecting of a union of divine particles. For the Hasidim, prayer (and love) was the necessary solution to isolation. It was the inevitable response of the divine in man which found solitude unbearable. It was the reaching out for fellowship, for roots.[5] (Dr. Eric Fromm has expressed in psycho-analytic terms this Hasidic viewpoint).[6]

The Hasidim were somewhat opposed to the Talmudists of their day, for the latter taught that God's will could only be determined through the meticulous study of the law. The Hasidim taught that the most uneducated man knew in his heart what God wanted. One Master taught, "There are some (the scholars) who have the key to the lock on the gate of Heaven, but God prefers that the lock be smashed with one heart-felt sigh!"[7] The Hasidim, like the authors of the Psalms, believed in the greater significance of the religion of the heart, rather than the religion of the mind. They believed with Bachya that the religious and more exalted nature of man was *latent in his soul* and awaited only the proper stimulus and channel of release. Further, the Hasidim taught that men could learn as much (or more) from the book of life as from the sacred literature. For them, nature, and especially human beings, were the best re-vealers of the divine miracles. For the Hasidim, the way to bind yourself to God was to bind yourself to nature and especially, to living things.

Modern teachers strongly support this view. One writes, "God is not an idea to be talked about so much as a personal reality to be experienced. He comes to persons through other persons. He is present wherever there is a loving relationship between human beings."[8] This is the central teaching of Martin Buber, who has been mediating the teaching of Hasidism to the modern world for fifty years. Hasidism taught that men reveal the nature of the divine within them by what they say, by their deeds, by their movements, even by their appearance. "Most of our fundamental religious teaching," says Dr. Miller,[9] "is not our conscious effort to tell the child anything, but is the unconscious and undesigned activities of the parents whose principles propagate themselves even without their desire."

Dr. Miller goes on to say a child first encounters God in his daily life "through the love shown to him by his parents." Thus parents become "mediators of God to their children" simply by loving them "long before any words are possible." The accumulated knowledge of modern psychology confirms what the Hasidim knew two centuries ago.

For the Talmudists, study was the necessary preparation for the meeting with God that we call prayer. The law was the vestibule down which one must walk before he could confront the king. The Hasidim emphasized the fact that men had a "way of knowing" that was prior to, perhaps even superior to, the intellectual understanding of God. They taught that it was possible to reach God and to be at one with Him, even without a detailed study of the law, provided that one practiced the indispensable virtue-love. Once, a disciple asked the maggid of Zlotchov, "How is it that the tradition holds that our Father Abraham kept all the laws, when most of the laws later given to Moses were unknown to Abraham?" The maggid answered, "All that is needed is to love God. If you are about to do something and you think it might lessen your love, then you will know it is sin. If you are about to do something and think it will increase your love, then you will know that your will is in keeping with the will of God. That is what Abraham did."[10]

We might say that, in essence, the Talmudists stood for the intellectual love of God, the Hasidim for the emotional love of God. In modern times, it is perhaps the attitude of the Hasidim that we need most. The Talmudists have much to teach us, namely, that where our orientation towards God is too abstract and mystical, it can evaporate into meaningless vapor. On the other hand, the Hasidim can teach us that in a scientifically oriented world which views most things mechanistically, we deeply need a sense of a personal relationship to our Creator and to our fellows.[11]

2. The Uniqueness of Each Person

> O sing unto the Lord a new song; for He hath
> done marvelous things. . . .
> (Psalm 98:1 *Union Prayerbook,* p. 48)

The Talmudists taught, "Study the Torah," discuss it, expound it, reflect upon it, and the divine word in it will be revealed to you. The Hasidim taught "Study man," especially the righteous man, the "Tzaddik." Listen to his words, observe his deeds, watch the way he moves, listen to the sound of his voice, touch him, imitate him, bind yourself to him, and link other men to yourself. The Talmudists taught, "Follow and understand the law, and you will walk the path of God." The Hasidim taught, "Don't simply imitate Moses. Seek your individual greatness. Express the unique greatness in yourself. After all, this is how Moses found his way to God. He did not simply imitate his fathers. He found his own way to God." The maggid of Zlotchov said, "Just as our fathers invented new ways of serving God, each a new service according to his own character, one the service of love, the other that of stern justice, the third that of beauty, *so each one of us in his own way shall devise something new in the light of the teachings and of service (ahvodah-worship-service), and do what has not yet been done.*"[12]

Once Rabbi Rafael asked Rabbi Pinhas, "Why is no human face like any other?" Rabbi Pinhas replied: "Because Man is created in the image of God. *Every human being sucks the living strength of God from another place,* and all together they make up Man. That is why their faces all differ from one another."[13] Rabbi Pinhas further said, "In every one there is something precious, which is in no one else. That is why it is said: 'Despise not any man.'" He taught, ". . . The dignity of a palace is no greater than that of a hut, for the two are not alike, and what the lesser accomplishes, the greater cannot. It is the same with the righteous man. Though his value and service be great, he cannot accomplish what the wicked man accomplishes in the hour he prays, or does something to honor God . . ."[14]

It is our heritage from the Hasidim that prayer is, then, intensely personal, but since the divinity in each person is only a fragment of the divinity found in others, prayer necessarily touches upon and involves all other human beings. Rabbi Pinhas taught, "a prayer which is not spoken in the name of the entire

85

community is no prayer at all."[15] That is to say, *a prayer which does not recognize the interdependence and inter-connectedness of all men is not a prayer, for it does not seek to unite the various unique fragments of divinity.* Since prayer is the uniting element in existence, since it is the expression of the divinity within ourselves, it partakes of the nature of divinity. Some of the Hasidim went so far as to say, "Prayer, in itself, is God."[16]

The leader of Hasidism considered the knowledge of Torah as only the beginning of the kind of knowledge God wished men to have. Like Bachya in the 11th century, the Baal Shem Tov taught that *beyond the Torah, there is the deeper knowledge that is latent in men's souls, which lies waiting to come into active reality.* The story is told that on Simchat Torah (the Festival of the Rejoicing of the Law), the Baal Shem Tov danced together with his congregation. (Group dancing was a feature of this folk religion.) He took the Scroll of the Torah and danced with it. Then he laid the Scroll aside and danced without it. At this moment, one of his disciples . . . said to his companions, "Now our master has laid aside the visible dimensional teachings, and has taken the spiritual teachings unto himself."[17] For the Hasidim, the Torah was the beginning. In the end, it was important that each man himself be a Torah, that is, a body of principles and experience, tied to God, from which other men might learn.

D. JOINING PRAYER AND DEED

Thou livest within our hearts, as Thou dost
    pervade the world,
And we through righteousness behold Thy
    presence.

(*Union Prayerbook,* p. 39)

How does one get into the mood to pray? How does one prepare to meet God? There is a story told about the Tzaddik of Nemirov which supplies an answer. A "mitnaggid," or an opponent to Hasidism, doubted the stories told about the piety of the Tzaddik. To find out for himself the truth of the stories, the Jew hid under the bed of the Tzaddik on the night set aside for the recitation of the Penitential Prayers offered before Rosh Hashanah (S'lichot). Came the time for prayer, the Tzaddik arose, performed his ablutions, and then, surprisingly, dressed in the garments of a peasant. The man under the bed had assumed that the Tzaddik would dress like a king before prayer. Then, the Tzaddik took an ax and left the house. The scoffer followed. The Tzaddik walked to a forest, chopped some wood laboriously, corded it into a bundle, shouldered it, and reentered the town. The investigator saw the Tzaddik stop at a small hut and tap at a window. When the sick widow was unable to open the door, the Tzaddik let himself in, and offered to "sell" her the wood for which she had no money. She could repay him "when" she had the money. He laid the wood in the stove and lit the fire. As he did so, he recited the first part of the prayers. When the wood burned cheerily, he recited the second part. As the fire warmed the house, he concluded the third part of the prayers. Henceforth, when he heard people say of the Tzaddik that he ascends to heaven when he prays, the investigator would add, "If not higher!"[18]

The Jewish tradition is certain of one thing. *Prayers must not be abstract. They must be preparation for or linked to work in behalf of oneself or others.* They are a part of ahvodah-service to the divine. The Talmud is equally clear on this point. It says, ". . . With what is he to be compared whose wisdom exceeds his works? With a tree whose branches are many, but whose roots are few . . . But what does he resemble whose works exceed his wisdom? A tree whose branches are few, but whose roots are many; the stormiest winds may bear down and rage upon it, but they cannot stir it from its place . . ."[19] When prayer and the prayerful-deed occur in close association, we have the "prayer-state" typical of a truly great man. The least of us is capable of this service (avodah) to God and to man.

E. THY WILL BE DONE

Draw our spirits toward Thee, and let Thy truth lead us. Help us to become instruments of Thy will.

(*Union Prayerbook*, pp. 27–28)

It is not impossible to reconcile the rabbinic and Hasidic approach to Judaism. There were Talmudists who recognized the need for the expression of the emotional God-orientation, and there were Hasidim who recognized the importance of the knowledge of the law as an anchor to society. Both the Talmudists and the Hasidim pursued the "will of God" but, generally speaking, the former made contact with God's will through the law derived from an original revelation, and the Hasidim stressed the significance of each human personality as a unique residence of the divine. One Hasidic Rabbi, Rabbi Mikhal of Zlotchov, commented on a verse from the Song of Songs (7:11), in this manner. The verse reads, "I am my beloved's, and his desire is toward me." The Rabbi taught (in paraphrase), "When man surrenders his selfish desires and seeks to serve God's broader will, then God's desire turns toward him."[20] The implication of this teaching is that when we subordinate our personal desires to the welfare of the community, we are helping to make real our new expanded desires. In brief, when we make God's cause our own, we are saying, "Thy will be done." Conversely, when we make His will our own, we have so joined ourselves to the divine that we have joined the force of God to the answering of our will. Then, indeed, "His desire is toward me." Here, again, prayer is conceived as a uniting force, uniting the will of man and God for the common good.

Bachya is right. "The study of the Torah is as tillage is to the soil—ploughing and clearing it." Praying is not merely a matter of plugging in to the ever-present electrical current. One must prepare for the encounter with the greater reality by studying exalted literature, by looking into one's own soul, and by examination of the living world around us. The word of God is revealed in the inspired wisdom of the historic past, in the deeper recesses of the human soul, and in the wonder of the physical world around us. We might here remind ourselves of Einstein's thought, "To know that which is impenetrable to us really exists, manifesting itself as the highest wisdom and the most radiant beauty which our dull faculties can comprehend only in their most primitive forms; this knowledge, this feeling, is at the center of true religiousness."[21] The person who wishes to pray, like Abraham and the Talmudist, like the Psalmist, Einstein, and Wordsworth, goes in search of the highest wisdom and seeks to unveil the deepest mystery, although he knows that he can never understand but primitively. For the religious person, a brief insight, a partial penetration, a momentary experience becomes the basis for an enduring and sustaining faith "that all which we behold is full of blessings," and that behind the blessings is a living Friend.

VII

Praying Together

I rejoiced when they said unto me: Let us go
unto the house of the Lord.

(Psalm 122:1 *Union Prayerbook,* p. 114)

A. FORMAL PRAYER

THE BOOK OF DANIEL INFORMS US THAT DANIEL, WHO LIVED IN
the second or third century B.C.E., prayed three times daily.[1] We
know that for well over two thousand years, Jews have had a
fixed prayer form to be recited morning, afternoon, and evening.
To be sure, there have always been many Jews, great leaders
among them, who have stressed the superior value of the spontaneous prayer, but *in addition to the spontaneous prayer,* traditional Jews have followed the pattern of the fixed prayers.

The last two centuries have witnessed a gradually deepening
revolt in the western world against ritual and formalism in religion, but there is a great deal to be said for the value of fixed
prayer. We have spoken of the content of some of the prayers in
the ancient Jewish Prayer-Book which still form the core of all
synagogue worship today. First, the prayers recognize God as
the Creator of all things. Then, we express our understanding
that His motivation for the creation was and is the love of His
children. We proceed to declare that He is one, the inference
being that all men are His children, therefore subject to one law,
and bound together by a common parenthood. Then, we are
bidden to love Him, just as He loves us, and we are told that we
can express this love by meditating upon His laws and by teaching and practicing them. With this foundation established, the
body of traditionally fixed prayer, then, includes a number of
specific "b'rachot" or "blessings," expressing our gratitude to
God for His many gifts, and soliciting His continued gifts of
peace, health, and redemption (both personal and societal;
redemption is understood in this-worldly terms.)[2] The Reform
Prayer-Book includes the prayers described above as part of the

basic foundation but selects only a few of the remaining prayers for recitation, emphasizing the universalistic content of the original prayer form.[3] All Jewish worship services end with prayers involving the worshiper in the labor for a world of brotherly love and peace.

Today, Orthodox Jews continue the requirement of formal prayers and synagogue attendance three times a day, while Reform Jews encourage spontaneous prayer on a daily basis and strongly urge attendance at the synagogue on Friday and holiday nights and Saturday and holiday mornings. (For most Reform congregations, Friday night is the major weekly service. A handful of Reform congregations still have their major service on Sunday mornings. Of late, many Reform congregations are instituting the daily morning and evening services.)

Whether Orthodox, Reform or Conservative, all Jewish congregations support the notion of fixed prayer at some time in the week. There is, to be sure, a wide range of difference in the content of the service and in the quantity of prayers, but all agree that modern man can benefit by regularly halting his whirlwind routine at a fixed moment to meditate on his relationship to the divine. If the content of the service is intelligently approached by the service-attender, he cannot help but gain something there to help him in facing his life problems.

1. Repentance (T'shuvah); Returning to the Task; Collective Sin

Our tradition makes it clear that prayer is but one of three things necessary for the religious person. The trinity of requirements includes Repentance, Prayer, and Charity.[4] Repentance in Judaism is a simple thing. It includes the elements of prayer and charity, just as each of these things includes elements of the other two. The repentant person is taught in Judaism to confess his sins (to God, no intermediary is needed) and to prepare himself to redirect the path of his life towards the moral law (Torah). These two aspects of the process of repentance are the prayer aspects. Then, the sinner is required to live the life of righteousness. The proof of his repentance is his return to the observance of the law. Indeed, the word for repentance in Judaism, is "T'shuvah," or "Return." For us, the forgiveness of God is always assured for the one who sincerely returns to the good life. Here, again, the constancy of God is assumed, and the changeableness of man is hoped for.[5]

The interesting thing, however, about the Jewish prayer-service is that it contains elements of a group confessional, not only on the High Holidays, but also in the daily service.[6] Judaism assumes that the "righteous" are not as righteous as they seem, that, indeed, they are partially responsible for the errors of the "wicked." On the other hand, Judaism assumes that the "wicked" are not as evil as they seem, and that their errors are, in part, the result of interaction with other people, who, in subtle ways, have contributed to the performance of the "sins." Thus, our fixed prayer-forms require the congregation to confess its errors together, as if each is guilty of the errors of all, and the group is guilty as a unit. This is a unique feature of the Jewish Service, and it indicates a realistic appraisal of the actions of men. The errors of the children are frequently the result of the absence of love in the family household, and the crimes committed by a member of a minority group, for example, are frequently tied to the oppression and discrimination he receives from the "righteous" members of the majority group. We are all responsible together for the sins of collective man, says Judaism. How could we pray this way without learning something profound that better equips us to return to our daily tasks?

Of course, the recitation of formal prayers can have a negative effect if the worshiper feels that in so doing, he substantially fulfills his duty to God and to man. The purpose of all prayer, including the formal prayer, is to lift and inspire. *Prayer is a first step in a process, a preparation for the deed of righteousness, the deed that unites man and God.* Its purpose is to help the individual attain to his own creative self, so that he might become a full partner in constructing the good society. The "worshiper" who leaves a formal religious service and says to himself, "It is done," has taken a step backward, not a step forward. He has deceived himself and blocked up the flowing channels of life. He is a worker in magic, not in religion.

2. The Fixed Time for Prayer; Prayer and Ritual

While there is always the danger that some people will misunderstand the purpose of the formal religious service, the need for the formal service is becoming an increasing necessity in our society, where everything is allotted a time in the appointment book except the meditative moment. It is "dinner at eight," "theatre at 8:45," "hairdresser at three," "tea at four," "board meeting at nine." The pace is truly hectic, but what time is set aside for the moment of communion with one's better self and with God? There are even planned "coffee-breaks," but the "spiritual-break" is neglected. Unless modern man plans a specific appointment for searching for his deeper meaning, he will live only on the periphery of life. He will live like the trained seal, in captivity, completely unaware that instead of performing his tricks on schedule, he could be plumbing the depths of exciting waters. Reform Judaism has had considerable success with its emphasis on the Friday evening service as the "fixed time" for prayer. More and more, Jews are responding to this "appointment." The value of service attendance, however, is to be measured not in terms of the number of people in the pews, but in terms of the work done by the attendees within themselves and in relation to their fellow human beings.

Orthodox religions attribute to rituals, divine sanction. The suggestion is that the rituals have, within themselves, a saving grace. Reform Judaism does not understand ritual in this way. We conceive of rituals as being man-made. We believe that God does not demand the performance of rituals, but He does wish us to ". . . do justly, and to love mercy, and to walk humbly with thy God" (Micah 6:8). None the less, ritual does have a place even in a religion which is primarily ethically oriented. We recognize the validity of a ritual when it helps to convey an idea or an emotion which it is otherwise difficult to express in a manner which all can comprehend. The recitation of the prayer over the wine on the Sabbath, for example, (*Union Prayerbook*, p. 93) is a ritual designed to remind us that the power which makes for freedom and for creation is always with us. The Synagogue Service, itself, is a kind of composite ritual and it serves not merely to convey intellectual notions but as a vehicle for the expression of emotions buried deep within the hearts of those who come to pray.

One does not have to believe that ritual is pleasing to God to understand its usefulness within certain bounds. This writer has often had worshipers speak to him in this vein, "Rabbi, I like the Hebrew prayers better than the English prayers. Not because I understand the Hebrew; I do not. Somehow, I can say things in Hebrew that I cannot say in English." This may sound like confused talk. It is not. This worshiper is merely saying that his subconscious is able to release its feelings better in non-intellectual sounds than in words which convey specific intellectual meanings. We, who accent the meaning of prayer as a conscious effort to enable us to grow towards the divine, would do well not to depreciate the meaning of the emotionally rooted prayer which surges up from the deeper wellsprings of our being. They may be the most meaningful prayers of all. Their expression in a language of undefined syllables could lead to the most profound development later on.

Reform Judaism has performed a great service for the modern Jew by relieving the Jewish community of the burden of an excessive ritualism. Now that we have absorbed this accomplishment, we are reassessing the value of a certain amount of ritual which is presented merely as an aid in the communication of the basic ideas of our faith. If we assume from the beginning that ritual for ritual's sake is superstition, we can still consciously use certain selected rituals to give our ideas the motor power that the emotions generate. An increasing number of Reform congregations are encouraging their members to recite the Sabbath prayers over the candles, over the wine, and over the bread. If one is prepared to limit the compelling nature of ritual, he can profit from the catalytic usefulness of Sabbath candles, Passover matzah, and fasting on Yom Kippur. The observance of these rituals, and the recitation of the prayers accompanying them, do not, in themselves, make us good Jews, but they can help us to our objective. They can be symbols and reminders of our plan to imitate the divine.

3. "Nothing Happens"—The Unmoved Soul

Loyalty to the system of fixed prayers can, of course, go to an undesirable extreme. The Talmudic Rabbis themselves argued against making a fetish of routine prayers. Rabbi Simion said, "When thou prayest, do not make the prayer a form of routine. Let it be rather an appeal to God for mercy and grace (Pirke Avot 2:18). Rabbi Eliezer ben Hyrcanus said on his deathbed, "When you pray, realize before whom you stand." We must bear in mind that the fixed prayer is not a prayer, in the highest sense of that term, unless the worshiper makes it his own. The worshiper, it is hoped, will first study the prayer which is the product of the genuine prayer experience of others before him, and, then, put himself in the mood of the prayer. He must, in the ideal relationship, feel the presence of the divine as he speaks the words. What did the poet say,

> "Listen, the mighty being is awake!
> and doth . . . make a sound like thunder
> everlasting!"[7]

It is this mood of awareness for which the worshiper must strive. The fixed prayer must be an incentive to personal awareness, a priming of the pump of feeling, or it is merely a collection of words. The person who says, "I come to services, read the prayers, and nothing happens," is merely revealing the fact that he has done nothing himself to permit the words to awaken thoughts and emotions within himself. This kind of person can also behold a glorious sunset and complain, "nothing happens." This person suffers from spiritual drought. He needs to dig deeply into the rock encrusted around his spirit before the well that is certainly within him can bubble up and work its wonders. In Bachya's image, he needs to polish the metal of his soul before it will reflect the divine. Only the person who comes to the altar of God with an awakened sensitivity, experiences "something happening."

4. "The Hour of Feeling"

The prayer hour on the Sabbath should be considered the time for piercing to the core of things. It should be shock treatment, reawakening us to the basic realities. It should be what the poet calls the "hour of feeling":

> "Love, now a universal birth,
> From heart to heart is stealing,
> From earth to man, from man to earth;
> —It is the hour of feeling.
>
> One moment now may give us more
> Than years of toiling reason;
> Our minds shall drink at every pore
> The spirit of the season.

Some silent laws ours hearts will make,
Which they shall long obey;
We for the years to come may take
Our temper from today.

And from the blessed power that rolls
About, below, above,
Will frame the measure of our souls:
They shall be turned to love."[8]

B. DEDICATION TO GROUP GOALS

Our sages taught that when one witnesses lightning, comets, thunder, hurricanes, or the like, he should pray, "Blessed is He whose almighty power fills the world."[9] The same men who found the evidence of God everywhere taught the value of the formal prayer. A man can pray well and deeply when he finds God for himself through nature or through spiritual reflection, but there is another profound meaning of prayer when it is performed in association with other human beings who have come together with the avowed intention of searching as a group for the deeper meaning of life.[10] Clinical psychological tests clearly show that a decision reached by a group can be more binding on each of the participants than a decision reached by an individual acting alone. There are decisions to be made when one is alone, and there are decisions which are best made by the group. Anyone who has felt the warmth and good-fellowship present at a congregational service, anyone who has witnessed the sharing of sorrow at a funeral, or the sharing of joy at a wedding, knows that there are things best accomplished in a group situation. The man who feels that he cannot reach God when he is alone is lacking in probing powers which must be trained and sharpened, but the person who feels that he does not need to share the aspirations and moods of the group is deceiving himself. Rabbi Mikhal prayed, "I join myself to all of Israel, to those who are more than I, that through these my thought may rise, and to those who are less than I, so that they may rise through my thought."[11] There is a special quality to group prayer from which all men can benefit.

Our Sages taught that God proclaimed, "He who prays with a congregation is credited with redeeming Me and My children."[12] This teaching reflects the strong Jewish conviction against the fragmentation of the community by those who flee from community responsibility and insist that they can gain nothing from the group. He who wishes to serve God cannot do so merely by staying out of trouble. He can "redeem" God only by working and praying with the community.

Our Sages also taught that certain prayers such as the "K'dushah, Sanctification" should not be recited by the individual alone. They were properly recited only in a group. Why did they come to this conclusion? Scripture teaches, "I will be hallowed among the children of Israel,"[13] (i.e., not by one child, not by an individual alone, but by the group acting in concert).

In this day, when there are strong pressures upon men to "go it" alone, we need the Synagogue more than ever. Our fathers were wise enough to know that when men pray together, they are less apt to engage in flights of fancy; they are less apt to pray selfishly; and they are the more easily reminded of their covenantal task. When men pray only when they are alone, they are not able to recite meaningfully the prayer which comes as the climax of our religious service, "Fervently we pray that day may come when all men, . . . created in Thine image, shall recognize that they are brethren . . ." (*Union Prayerbook,* p. 71). The ultimate goal of prayer is to unite the hearts of men. Indeed our Prayer Book reads, "Unite our hearts, that we may serve thee *in truth*."[14]

VIII

Giving Strength to God

JUDAISM HAS TAUGHT THAT NOT ONLY DO MEN GIVE STRENGTH TO each other, but righteous men help to give God strength. The mass slaughter of millions of Jews in World War II, like other human catastrophies, underscores the fact that the inhumanity of man to man is a betrayal of God. God must have human agents to administer laws rooted in His nature. Righteous men project His power into the world. He must have mediators and intercessors as Moses and Jeremiah classically demonstrated. This viewpoint has been ably presented by my revered teacher, Dr. Henry Slonimsky, who has written, "They (i.e., man and God) become allies in the most redoubtable of all struggles and for the greatest of all stakes. . . . But in a very real sense, the fate of God and of the future rests on the heroism of man, on what he elects to do, for he is . . . the focus of decision."[1]

The Maggid of Zlotchov expounded on the verse, "Ye shall be holy; for I, the Lord, your God, am holy."[2] He taught, "This is what is meant: *'My holiness,' which is the world, depends upon your holiness.* As you sanctify My name below, so it is sanctified in the heights of Heaven. For it is written: *'Give ye strength unto God.'* "[3]

Prayer, then, is not merely a one-way street. It is a vehicle through which man and God strengthen each other, as men and God, together, sanctify the world by serving each other. God has His work, as witness the endless power which He pipes into the universe, but there are certain tasks reserved for man, which man alone can do and must do in moving the mutual cause forward. Dr. Slonimsky has written, "God hands a chalice to mankind which mankind must hand back to Him at the end of days, foaming with its own inner saps and juices, its own sweat and blood and wine, its own infinite experience."[4]

"Religion," wrote Montague,[5] "is a momentous possibility, the possibility namely that what is highest in spirit is also deepest in nature—that there is something at the heart of nature, something akin to us, a conserver and increaser of values . . . that the

things that matter most are not at the mercy of the things that matter least." Judaism suggests that this "something at the heart of nature" is concerned with us as individuals and that prayer is a yearning ". . . which God Himself puts into our hearts to give back to Him enriched by our fervor, our power."

"To act out of love," wrote Slonimsky, "and to be willing to bear the suffering which the good and true man must inevitably bear in a world like ours, in a world which is only partly divine and which must be won for God through the efforts of man,— that is the deepest utterance of the rabbis and the culminating idea of Jewish religiosity and of Jewish prayer."[6]

Not God alone. Not man alone. But God and man together, interacting and tied together, in a never-ending process of prayer and work (*avodah*).

Bibliography

BAECK, DR. LEO. *God and Man in Judaism,* Union of American Hebrew Congregations, New York, 1958.

BERGMANN, HUGO, Ed., *Philo,* Philosophia Judaica, East and West Library, Oxford, 1946.

BIAL, RABBI MORRISON DAVID, *An Offering of Prayer,* Temple Sinai of Summit, Summit, New Jersey, 1962.

BRODY, H., Ed., *Selected Poems of Jehuda Halevi,* translated by Nina Salaman, The Jewish Publication Society of America, Philadelphia, 1946.

BUBER, MARTIN, *Hasidism and Modern Man,* Horizon Press, New York, 1958.

———, *Tales of the Hasidim, The Early Masters,* Schocken Books, Inc., New York, 1947.

———, *To Hallow This Life,* Harper and Brothers, New York, 1958.

BUBER, SOLOMON, Ed., *Midrash Tanhuma,* Poland Publishers, Wilna, 1885.

EPSTEIN, DR. I., Rabbi, Ed., B'rachot, "Berachoth," *The Babylonian Talmud,* Seder Zara'im, I, The Soncino Press, London, 1948.

FOSDICK, DR. HARRY EMERSON, *The Meaning of Prayer,* Associated Press, New York, 1949.

FRANKFORT, H. and H. A., J. A. WILSON, T. JACOBSEN, and WM. A. IRWIN, *The Intellectual Adventures of Ancient Man,* The University of Chicago Press, Chicago, Ill., 1946.

FREEHOF, SOLOMON, *The Small Sanctuary,* Union of American Hebrew Congregations, Cincinnati, 1942.

FRIEDMAN, MAURICE S., *Martin Buber: The Life of Dialogue,* The University of Chicago Press, Chicago, Ill., 1955.

FROMM, ERICH, *The Art of Loving,* Harper and Brothers, New York, 1956.

GITTELSOHN, ROLAND B., *Man's Best Hope,* Random House, New York, 1961.

GLATZER, NAHUM, *In Time and Eternity,* Schocken Books Inc., New York, 1946.

HEILER, FRIEDRICH, *Prayer: A Study in the History and Psychol-*

ogy of Religion, Ed. by Samuel McComb, Oxford University Press, N.Y., 1958. (See also, 1932 edition.)

HERTZ, DR. JOSEPH H., Ed., *The Authorized Daily Prayer Book,* Revised Edition, Bloch Publishing Co., New York, 1948.

The Holy Bible, Revised Standard Version, Thomas Nelson & Sons, New York, 1953.

The Holy Scriptures, According to the Masoretic Text, The Jewish Publication Society of America, Philadelphia, 1958.

IBN PAKUDA, BACHYA BEN JOSEPH, *Duties of the Heart* (Hovot Ha-L'vavot), five volumes, translation from the Arabic into Hebrew by Jehuda ibn Tibbon; English translation by Rev. Moses Hyamson, 1925, published by Bloch Publishing Co., New York, 1943.

JAMES, WILLIAM, *The Varieties of Religious Experience,* Longmans, Green and Co., London, New York, Toronto, 1929.

Midrash Rabbah, KTAV Publishing House, New York, NPD, Vol. I.

MILLER, DR. RANDOLPH C., *Your Child's Religion, A Practical Guide For Parents,* Doubleday, New York, 1962.

MINKIN, JACOB S., *The World of Moses Maimonides,* Thomas Yoseloff, New York, 1957.

MOORE, GEORGE FOOT, *Judaism,* Vol. II, Harvard University Press, Cambridge, 1950, especially the chapters on "Prayer" and "Study"; also Vol. I, 1927, on "The Idea of God," pp. 357–423.

NEWMAN, DR. LOUIS I., RABBI and SAMUEL SPITZ, *The Talmudic Anthology,* Behrman House, Inc., New York, 1945.

PARKER, WM. R. and ELAINE ST. JOHNS, *Prayer Can Change Your Life,* Prentice-Hall, Inc., Englewood Cliffs, New Jersey, 1957.

PHILIPSON, DAVID, *The Reform Movement in Judaism,* The Macmillan Co., New York, 1931.

PLAUT, DR. W. GUNTHER, RABBI, *Judaism and the Scientific Spirit,* Issues of Faith, Union of American Hebrew Congregations, New York, 1962.

SINGER, REV. S., translator, *The Standard Prayer Book,* Hebrew and English, Bloch Publishing Co., New York, 1951.

STEINBERG, DR. MILTON, RABBI, *Basic Judaism,* Harcourt, Brace and Company, New York, 1947.

SHOLEM, GERSHOM G., *Major Trends In Jewish Mysticism,* Schocken Books, Inc., New York, 1946.

The Torah, The Five Books of Moses, The Jewish Publication Society of America, Philadelphia, 1962.

Union Prayerbook, for Jewish Worship, Newly Revised, Part I, published by The Central Conference of American Rabbis, New York, 1961.

Pamphlets and Articles

Borowitz, Dr. Eugene, Rabbi, "The Idea of God," *Yearbook*, Central Conference of American Rabbis, Philadelphia, 1957, Vol. LXVII, pp. 174–186.

"Commentary to the *Union Prayerbook*," Preliminary Draft, Central Conference of American Rabbis, The Liturgy Committee, 1960.

Eisenstein, Judah D., the article "Prayer," in the Jewish Encyclopedia, Funk and Wagnalls Co., (New York and London, 1905), Vol. X, pp. 164 ff.

Klausner, Samuel Z., "Worship," UAHC, N.Y., 1959.

Mihaly, Eugene, "Religious Experience in Judaism," The Rydal Press, Keighley, Yorks, Great Britain, 1957.

Ostrow, Mortimer, M. D., "The Psychology of Religious Worship: A Project," Conference on Worship Research, Union of American Hebrew Congregations, New York, N.Y., Feb. 1959.

Slonimsky, Dr. Henry, "The Philosophy Implicit in the Midrash," HUC Annual, Vol. XXVII, 1956, pp. 251 ff.

————, "Prayer," a pamphlet, published by Temple Israel, South Orange, N.J., 1953.

Notes

The Sephardic pronunciation is used for Hebrew transliteration. The "sh'va" is usually represented by an apostrophe ('). The "patach" and "kamatz" are reproduced as (a), the "kamatz katan" as (o). The "tzere" is usually reproduced as (e) as in "bed." The "chet" and "chaf" are both rendered as (ch) except in the case of "Hasidism," where common usage dictated the retention of the (ḥ).

INTRODUCTION

1. This is a paraphrase of a teaching by the "Baal Shem Tov," Rabbi Israel ben Eliezar, based on an incident recorded by Martin Buber, *Tales of The Hasidim, The Early Masters,* Schocken Books, Inc., N.Y., 1947, p. 48.
2. *Ibid.* pp. 2–3.
3. *Ibid.* pp. 2–3.
4. *Ibid.* p. 125. Rabbi Pinhas of Koretz said, "But he who knows that prayer in itself is God, is like the King's son who takes whatever he needs from the stores of his father." See now, Friedrich Heiler, *Prayer: A Study in the History and Psychology of Religion,* translated by Samuel Mc-Comb, Oxford University Press, New York, 1958, p. 108, "The truly and deeply religious man . . . feels that his praying is not his own work . . . but . . . streams out of the plentitude and power of God. . . . The mysterious impulse which drives him to prayer is the revelation of the indwelling God at work in the deepest places of his soul."
5. William James, *The Varieties of Religious Experience,* Longmans, Green and Co., London, N.Y., Toronto, 1929, p. 508.
5A. See now the teaching of Ibn Pakuda, ". . . the soul . . . inclines to what resembles it. . . . And when the soul apprehends aught that will bring more light and vigor to herself, she will turn to it in her musings, attach herself to it in her thought and represent it to herself in her imagination. She will desire it and yearn for it . . . ," *Duties of the Heart,* Bachya ben Joseph ibn Pakuda, English translation by Moses Hyamson, Bloch Publishing Co., N.Y., 1947, Volume V, Tenth Treatise on "Love of God," page 28.
6. See the article by Lawrence A. Block, "The Personal God Idea in Reform Judaism," Central Conference of American Rabbis Journal, New York, January, 1962, Vol. IX, No. 4, pp. 7–15. In the 1937 Columbus platform, the Rabbis expressed their belief in God as the "ideal of conduct."
7. Genesis 1:26. All biblical citations are from *The Holy Scriptures According to the Masoretic Text,* the Jewish Publication Society of America, Phila., 1958.

8. *Midrash Rabbah,* "KTAV" Publishing House, New York, NPD, Vol. I, 8:8, p. 15b. This interpretation is implied in R. Simlai's response to his disciples after they rejected his answer to the minim. (I am indebted to Dr. Eugene Mihaly, of the Hebrew Union College-Jewish Institute of Religion, Cincinnati, for drawing this to my attention.)

9. *The Union Prayerbook for Jewish Worship,* newly revised, Central Conference of American Rabbis, Part I, N.Y., 1958, p. 147. See our note 21, Chap. IV and Philo's comment that the voice of God is *visible.*

10. Elizabeth Barrett Browning, "Grief," *The Home Book of Verse,* Ed. by Burton E. Stevenson, sixth edition, Henry Holt and Co., N.Y., 1930, p. 3353. The poem begins, "I tell you hopeless grief is passionless; that only men, etc."

11. Actually, "Asir Tikvah," *Selected Poems of Jehudah Halevi,* translated by Nina Salaman, Ed. by H. Brody, The Jewish Publication Society of America, Phila., 1946, p. 96.

12. Our Prayer Book frequently uses this phrase. See *UPB,* pp. 23, 139.

CHAPTER I

1. This emphasis is not absent from our tradition. It was evident in the "Pittsburgh Platform" in 1885, as adopted by Reform leaders. See *The Reform Movement in Judaism,* David Philipson, The Macmillan Co., New York, 1931, pp. 355 ff. For a more recent treatment of the subject, see "The Idea of God," Rabbi Dr. Eugene Borowitz, *Yearbook,* Central Conference of American Rabbis, Phila., 1957, Vol. LXVII, pp. 174–186. An important discussion on "The Idea of God" is to be found in *Judaism,* G. F. Moore, Harvard University Press, Cambridge, 1927, Vol. I., pp. 357–423. See also *Basic Judaism,* Dr. Milton Sternberg, Harcourt, Brace and Company, New York, 1947, pp. 31–63, and *God and Man in Judaism,* Dr. Leo Baeck, Rabbi, Union of American Hebrew Congregations, New York, 1958.

2. The article on "Prayer" by Judah D. Eisenstein, in *The Jewish Encyclopedia,* Funk and Wagnalls Co., New York and London, 1905, Vol. X, pp. 164 ff., is most informative. See now, p. 166 there, "The word 'tefilah' is defined as 'thought' and 'hope,' as representing the means of reasoning and discriminating between good and evil." Many of the traditional prayers are appeals for "wisdom" and "discernment." See also the *Authorized Daily Prayer Book,* revised edition, Ed. by Dr. Joseph H. Hertz, Bloch Publishing Co., N.Y., 1948, p. xi, where "tefilah" or "prayer" is said to come from the root meaning "to judge" or "self-examination."

3. The translators of *The Torah, The Five Books of Moses,* The Jewish Publication Society of America, Phila., 1962, assure us that this concept is post-biblical.

4. Psalm 29:11.

CHAPTER II

1. "What I Believe," *Forum Magazine,* Oct., 1930. See now the teaching of Rabbi Levi Yitzchak, *Tales of the Hasidim,* p. 232, "However

much a man may learn, he should always remember that he has not even gotten to the first page."

2. These words were originally expressed by the Seer, Balaam, when he blessed Israel in the name of God. For Balaam, the moment of revelation-discovery involved his beholding the greatness of the people Israel (Numbers 23:23).

3. Job 42:5.

4. Wordsworth, "Lines Composed a Few Miles Above Tintern Abbey."

5. Wordsworth, *Ibid.*

6. *Ibid.*

7. Shakespeare, "As You Like It," Act II, Scene I, spoken by Duke Senior. His speech begins, "Now, my co-mates and brothers in exile . . ." The Duke contends that even adversity has its blessings.

CHAPTER III

1. Genesis 1:26, 27.

2. I heard this from my father. A similar idea is found in *In Time and Eternity,* N. Glatzer, Schocken Books, Inc., N.Y., 1946, p. 23. This has the ring of the statement of Rabbi Pinhas of Koretz quoted here in note 4, cf. of the saying of Rabbi Barukh, *Tales of the Hasidim,* pp. 89–90, "Do not think that you cannot be redeemed. . . . Every man has the vocation of making perfect something in this world."

3. Genesis 1:26–27.

4. This is a summary view as implied in the teaching that the God who created the world made a covenant with Israel and hears the prayers of men. See now Solomon's prayer at the dedication of the first Temple (I Kings 8:27 ff.), "But will God in very truth dwell on the earth? behold, heaven and the heaven of heavens cannot contain thee; how much less this house that I have builded! Yet have thou respect unto the prayer of thy servant, and to his supplication, O Lord, my God, to hearken unto the cry and to the prayer which thy servant prayeth before Thee this day. . . ."

5. *UPB,* pp. 12, 29, 51, 64, 118, 186, etc. This is the prayer immediately following the "call to prayer" which begins, "Bor'chu et Adonai ha-m'vorach."

6. *UPB,* pp. 12, 64, 119, 186, etc. The traditional prayer book follows this procedure even more consistently.

7. *UPB,* pp. 14, 30, 52, 66, 120, 188, etc.

8. Hosea 11:4 following Professor William A. Irwin, *Intellectual Adventures of Ancient Man,* H. Frankfort, etc., The University of Chicago Press, Chicago, 1946, p. 229; the standard usage is "bands of love."

9. Fromm, Erich, *The Art of Loving,* Harper and Brothers, N.Y., 1956, pp. 22–26.

10. *UPB,* pp. 13, 65, etc. The morning prayer is only slightly different.

11. *UPB,* pp. 14, 30, 52, 66, 120, 188, etc.

12. Exodus 19:18 ff.

13. Exodus 19:24–20:17. Note (Ex. 20:16, 17) that after Moses came down the people said to Moses, "Speak thou with us, and we will hear,

but let not God speak with us, lest we die." Moses speaks God's wishes in terms of the Commandments.

14. Exodus 32:1–2.

15. From the text alone (Ex. 32:1–6) it is possible to contend that the people were not worshiping a different God but were engaging in a form of worship not pleasing to the God of Israel (Ex. 32:7, 8).

16. The reader can learn much from a study of *The Small Sanctuary, Judaism In The Prayerbook,* Rabbi Dr. Solomon Freehof, UAHC, Cincinnati, 1942.

17. Deuteronomy 29:9–14. See now, especially, 29:13, 14. "Neither with you only do I make this covenant and this oath; but with him that standeth here with us this day, . . . and also with him that is not here with us this day. . . ."

18. *The Union Haggadah,* revised, Central Conference of American Rabbis, Cincinnati, 1923, pp. 20, 22. The exact rendering here is, "It is because of what the Lord did for *me* when I came forth out of Egypt." *cf.* p. 38, "not our fathers alone, but us also, did the Holy one redeem . . ."

19. Genesis 17:2–4.

20. Deuteronomy 29:13–14.

21. We do this by following his moral law (Deut. 30:10). Involved is man's *choice* of good rather than evil (30:15–20).

22. The concept of covenant implies that future generations are bound to the agreement entered into by their fathers. Jews today are under the commandment administered to the fathers. They cannot escape this moral responsibility.

23. Genesis 1:1–6:8, in the oldest tradition. The Reform tradition divides this reading into three parts.

24. Isaiah 42:6; "I, the Lord have called thee in righteousness, and have taken hold of thy hand, and kept thee, and set thee for a covenant of the people, for a light of the nations . . ." ('l'or goyim.")

25. St. Mark 15:34; St. Matthew 27:46.

26. Rabbi Levi Yitzchak, as quoted by M. Buber, *Tales of the Hasidim,* pp. 212–213.

27. Sanhedrin 37a, Chapter IV, Mishna 5. Actually ". . . one soul in Israel."

28. Tennyson, "Flower in the Crannied Wall."

29. The customary translation for the word "Elohim" here is "angels." See the Jewish Publication Society, *The Holy Scriptures,* Phila., 1955. *The Holy Bible,* Revised Standard Version, Thomas Nelson & Sons, New York, 1953, translates literally "God." There is less timidity among scholars generally today to translate the word for what it means, "God." See now William Irwin, *The Intellectual Adventures of Ancient Man,* U. of Chicago Press, Chicago, 1946, p. 258.

30. This is a summary statement for a viewpoint which dominates the Holy Scriptures.

31. See now, Rabbi Dr. Gunther Plaut, *Judaism and the Scientific Spirit,* Issues of Faith, Union of American Hebrew Congregations, New York, 1962. See especially Chapter VI, "The Search for Truth," pp. 66 ff.

32. Psalm 107:23 ff. seems to describe the seafaring man as being thus conscious of God at all times.

33. *UPB*, pp. 118, 219.

34. Genesis 1:28 ff., "And God blessed them. . . . 'Be fruitful, and multiply, and replenish the earth, and subdue it; and have dominion over the fish of the sea, and over the fowl of the air, and over every living thing. . . . Behold, *I have given you* . . .'" The gift is prior to the asking. (Italics mine.)

CHAPTER IV

1. Gen. 28:10–17.

2. Gen. 28:16.

3. Gen. 28:17.

4. The Hebrew word for angels means "messengers," (Gen. 28:12). The text reads, ". . . and behold the angels of God *ascending* and descending on it."

5. This story from Theodore Reik, *Myth And Guilt*, Braziller, New York, 1957.

6. Quoted here, Chapter III–A.

7. Jeremiah 2:12 "m'kor mayim chaim."

8. Gen. 21:14.

9. Gen. 21:16–18.

10. Gen. 21:19.

11. II Kings 6:14 ff.

12. II Kings 6:15.

13. II Kings 6:16.

14. II Kings 6:17.

15. *Ibid.*

16. II Kings 6:19–20.

17. *Tales of the Hasidim*, p. 130. Told of Rabbi Rafael of Bershad.

18. *Prayer*, F. Heiler, p. 65.

19. Rabbi Roland B. Gittelsohn in *Man's Best Hope*, Random House, New York, 1961, seems to support this view. See his discussion involving prayer, pp. 162–185. The Traditional Prayerbook suggests an abbreviated prayer in time of illness which includes the petition, "Even before we call, do Thou answer. Blessed art Thou, O Lord, who hearkenest unto prayer." The Hebrew begins, "Terem nikrah atah ta-a-ne . . ." *The Authorized Daily Prayer Book*, revised Edition, Edited by Dr. Joseph H. Hertz, Rabbi, Bloch Publishing Co., N.Y., 1948, p. 158. The Psalmist prayed (55:23), "Cast thy burden upon the Lord, and He will sustain thee. . . ."

20. From a "Lament for Lost Paradise" by Kathleen Raine, the *New Yorker Magazine*, June 9, 1962, p. 98.

21. Isaiah 65:24. Commenting on Ex. 20:18 (some texts 20:15), Philo says, "All the people saw the voice . . . it is the case that the voice of man is audible, but the voice of God truly visible. Why so? Because whatever God says is not words but deeds. . . ." *On the Decalogue*, 44–9 (vs.

11, pp. 29 ff.), quoted in Philo, *Philosophia Judaica,* Ed. Hugo Bergmann, East and West Library, Oxford, 1946, p. 78.

22. Quoted here, Chapter III–A.

23. Psalms 23:4.

24. *UPB,* pp. 77, 153.

25. This is to be compared to the saying of Rabbi Levi Yitzchak, quoted in *Tales of the Hasidim,* p. 213. See now, the quotation from Bachya in Ch. V, G of this paper.

26. *UPB,* pp. 118–119, 340–341.

27. *UPB,* p. 93. I have translated the Hebrew in a paraphrase. The thought is clearly there.

28. The "answer" of God is always there. We are not always able to "hear" it. See note 21 above. (The answer of God is *visible.*)

CHAPTER V

1. *The Meaning of Prayer,* by the Rev. Dr. Harry Emerson Fosdick, Association Press, N.Y., 1949, can be helpful to all. See pp. 34–35 there.

2. Leviticus 19:2.

3. See Philo on this thought, our note 21, Chap. IV. Man, too, reveals his real nature and beliefs by his deeds. Is not belief in God an inference from one's life? It can scarcely be measured by a mere verbal statement of belief.

4. *To Hallow This Life,* Martin Buber, Horizon Press, New York, 1958. See now, *Martin Buber: The Life of Dialogue,* ed. by Maurice S. Friedman, Chicago, 1955. Dr. Friedman quotes Buber, p. 242, "The great achievement of Israel is not so much that it has told man of the one, real God, the origin and goal of all that exists, but rather that it has taught men that they can address God in very reality, that men can say Thou to Him, that we human beings can stand face to face with Him, there is communion between God and man." The recognition of God, says Buber, is not limited to any one form, image, or manifestation, for He is everywhere. "Revelation is an *event* (italics this author's) which is *experienced* by an individual or a group of people as an *abiding astonishment* which no knowledge of causes can weaken, as wonder at something which intervenes fatefully in the life of this individual and this group, . . ." "Israel and the World," p. 97 f, cited by Friedman, p. 244. According to Buber, "My own belief in revelation . . . (is that) *we are revealed to ourselves*—and cannot express it otherwise than as something revealed," "Eclipse of God," p. 173 (italics mine).

5. This is part of a commentary on Ezekiel 3:12, which is quoted from the Zohar in *In Time and Eternity,* edited by Nahum N. Glatzer, Schocken Books Inc., New York, 1945, p. 31. This is also the substance of a commentary in *Midrash Tanhuma,* edited by Solomon Buber, Poland Publishers, Wilna, 1885, Yitro 17. The latter states, in effect, God reveals Himself "L'fi koho shel kol echad v'echad," according to each man's individual power. Cf. *The Talmudic Anthology,* Dr. Louis I. Newman, Rabbi and Samuel Spitz, Behrman House, Inc., New York, 1945, p. 151, top.

6. The projection which we make is towards a "more" of the same which we have experienced. Where our projection makes us aware of the greater power in the world, which solicits from us a greater hope and a greater desire to serve, we are reaching towards the reality which is God, although we can never encompass Him in totality.

7. Quoted here, Chapter III–A.

8. This is the opinion of the Baal Shem Tov, *Tales of the Hasidim,* p. 48.

9. *Ibid.* pp. 64–65.

10. This is from a discussion "On Hiding From the Presence of God," from *Legum Sacrarum Allegoriarum Libri* as quoted in *In Time and Eternity,* Nahum N. Glatzer, Schocken Books Inc., N.Y., 1946, p. 36. Philo used this teaching in the sense that the man who flees from God into himself is the one who claims that he himself is the cause of things that come to pass and not God. Philo does not mean to say that man has no role in creation. He is saying that we must link ourselves to the divine mind which created us, and of which we are a part. Actually, says Philo, since God is everywhere, it is impossible to hide from Him. To flee from Him is to flee to unreality. See further on this writing, *Judaism,* Harvard University Press, Cambridge, 1927, Vol. I, p. 372, and the comments by G. F. Moore.

11. As did the Prophet Elijah, I Kings 19:11 ff.

12. Gen. 24:63, *cf.* Psalm 19 on the glories of God's created things.

13. Job 38:1 ff.

14. "To a Skylark."

15. *UPB,* p. 51, cf. p. 29.

16. *Duties of the Heart,* Bachya ibn Pakuda, Vol. 1, p. 39, from the tractate, "The Service of God"; translated by Moses Hyamson, Bloch Publ. Co., N.Y., 1941.

17. B'rachot 30 b, 32 b.

18. *Sifre Deuteronomy* on Deut. 11:12, 41. Ed. Friedman, f. 80 a. See now the excellent chapter on "Study" in *Judaism,* Vol. II, George F. Moore, London, 1950, p. 240 ff.

19. B'rachot 63 a, commenting on Proverbs 3:6.

20. These quotations are parts of a chapter on "Study" by G. F. Moore, *Judaism,* Vol. II, Harvard University Press, Cambridge, 1950, pp. 239 ff. Our note is a reference to Moore's note 6, p. 242, concerning Ben Zoma; and his note 7, p. 242 concerning Johanan. See his references there.

21. See Chapter VI which follows Pirke Avot, attributed to R. Meir, as found in *The Authorized Daily Prayer Book,* S. Singer, Ninth American Edition, Hebrew Publishing Co., New York, 1914, pp. 204–205; *UPB,* p. 177.

22. From the prayer immediately following the "Sh'ma," *UPB,* p. 15, l'totafot ben enechah" (Deut. 6:8).

23. Gen. 12:1 ff.

24. Gen. 15:1 ff.; Gen. 17:1 ff.; Gen. 18:1 ff.

25. From the pamphlet, "Prayer," by Dr. Henry Slonimsky, p. 15, published by Temple Israel, South Orange, N.J. Dr. Slonimsky was for many years Dean of the Jewish Institute of Religion, New York (now the

Hebrew Union College–Jewish Institute of Religion). As Professor of Religion there, he inspired many students, including this author. Not all of the approaches in this book stem from Dr. Slonimsky's influence, but if a certain fervor is detected, this is the author's heritage from that master teacher.

26. That is, "Come . . . that thou mayest bring forth My people . . . out of Egypt," Exodus 3:10.
27. This is the substance of Amos 9:7.
28. This is the theme of the Book of Jonah.
29. *UPB*, pp. 15, 120, etc.
30. This is the import of Pirke Avot, 3:12. See *UPB*, pp. 171–2.
31. Introduction to *Duties of the Heart*, by Bachya, Vol. I, p. 18.
32. *Ibid.* See Vol. IV, "The Accounting of the Soul" (Cheshbon Hanefesh), p. 70.
33. *Ibid.* p. 106.

CHAPTER VI

1. *The Road to Successful Living*, Rabbi Louis Binstock, Simon and Schuster, N.Y. 1958, p. 294. Rabbi Binstock quotes, on p. 78, the prayer of a Rabbi afflicted with blindness, "Oh, God, we do not ask for perfect health, but for the power to transmute illness and affliction into service on Thy altar; we do not ask for perfect happiness, but rather for the power to shape suffering into service and tears into triumph of the spirit; we do not ask for a perfect world, but for the power to change and refashion it more clearly after Thy will . . ."
2. *Religion in a Changing World*, Rabbi Dr. Abba Hillel Silver, Harper, N.Y., 1930. The story is here paraphrased.
3. Or ". . . and we will be strengthened."
4. As quoted in *The World of Moses Maimonides*, Jacob S. Minkin, Thomas Yoseloff, New York, 1957, pp. 149–150. The authorship of the prayer is not certain. Dr. Joseph H. Hertz, Chief Rabbi of Great Britain, according to Mr. Minkin (*ibid.* p. 150) wrote Sir William Osler that the prayer is the product of a Dr. Markus Herz (1784–1803), a physician in the Jewish Hospital in Berlin. Others hold that the prayer shows the clear influence of Maimonides (see Minkin's discussion). For our purposes, it is unimportant which of these Jewish doctors wrote the prayer. It is the content of the prayer which commands our attention.
5. See the introduction to *Tales of the Hasidim*, especially pp. 3, 4. Buber writes there, "If you direct the undiminished power of your fervor to God's world-destiny, if you do what you must do at this moment—no matter what it may be!—with your whole strength and with kavvanah, with holy intent, you will bring about the union between God and Shekkinah, eternity and time." Then, Buber continues, "You need not be a scholar or a sage to accomplish this. *All that is necessary is to have a soul united within itself and indivisibly directed to its divine goal.*" (italics, mine).
6. See now, *The Art of Loving*, Dr. Erich Fromm, Harper and Bros.,

N.Y., 1956, p. 8, "The experience of separateness arouses anxiety; it is, indeed, the source of all anxiety. . . . The awareness of human separation, without reunion by love—is the source of shame. It is at the same time, the source of guilt and anxiety. . . . The deepest need of man, then, is the need to overcome his separateness, to leave the prison of his aloneness. . . ." The answer of the Hasidim of the 18th century is the answer of the 20th century psychiatrist. Humans must bind each other together with love.

7. *Tales of the Hasidim,* p. 64.
8. *Your Child's Religion, A Practical Guide for Parents,* Dr. R. C. Miller, Doubleday, New York, 1962, p. 23; cf. pp. 107–108.
9. *Ibid.* pp. 45–46.
10. *Tales of the Hasidim,* p. 149. "Maggid" means literally, "preacher, the one who tells," i.e., the "story," the story with the message of learning. Zlotchov, like most of the small towns where the Hasidim lived, was in Eastern Europe.
11. Hasidism emphasized the "joy" of the truly religious life. For a study of some of the mystic trends in Hasidism, which are not our primary concern here, see *Major Trends in Jewish Mysticism,* Gershom G. Sholem, Schocken Books, Inc., N.Y., 1946.
12. *Tales of the Hasidim,* p. 147.
13. *Ibid.* pp. 126, 127.
14. *Ibid.* p. 127.
15. *Ibid.* p. 126.
16. *Ibid.* p. 125.
17. *Ibid.* p. 53.
18. The story is told by I. L. Peretz, "Oib Nisht Noch Hecher." It is found in translation as "If not Higher," in *The Prince of the Ghetto,* Maurice Samuel, Alfred A. Knopf, New York, 1948, pp. 191 ff.
19. The Mishnaic tractate, Avot III ("Sayings of the Fathers"), see *UPB,* pp. 171–72.
20. *Tales of the Hasidim,* p. 149. A similar thought is expressed in Pirke Avot 2:4 "He used to say 'Make His will as thy will so that He may make thy will as His will.' "
21. Quoted here, Chapter III–A.

CHAPTER VII

1. Daniel 6:11. The biblical book tells us that Daniel prayed in this manner even in defiance of a royal decree.
2. Important is the prayer for "knowledge, understanding, and discernment," Singer, *The Standard Daily Prayer Book,* Bloch Publ. Co., N.Y., 1951, p. 56, see *UPB,* pp. 118–120.
3. Orthodox Judaism included prayers for all men, but emphasized the salvation of the Jewish community (i.e.—since the community and not the individual was the primary prayer unit, it was natural to include the community immediately involved, Israel). Reform Judaism, born in the 18th century, in an age of increasing democracy and universalism, re-

emphasized the message of the Hebrew Prophets of the 7–9th centuries B.C.E. and included another word or two in the ancient prayers, stressing the universalistic aspect of Judaism. Basically, the Reform (Union) Prayer Book leans heavily on the ancient prayers, and is original primarily, in its selectivity and emphasis. The *UPB* has made an important contribution to the development of Judaism in the translation of the Hebrew prayers into a poetic English suitable for prayer.

4. See *UPB*, II, pp. 256, 257.

5. The daily service contains a prayer for repentance, *Singer*, p. 56. In translation, it goes, in part, "Cause us to return, O our Father, unto Thy Law; draw us near, O our King, unto Thy service, and bring us back in perfect repentance unto Thy presence. Blessed art Thou, O Lord, who delightest in repentance." Note that the man who prays seeks to return to the *law* and to God's service. This involves active commitment on the part of the worshiper. See *UPB* (I), pp. 50, 296.

6. *Singer;* pp. 56, 67, and *UPB*, p. 296. The High Holiday prayer lists specific sins for all to confess together. See The High Holiday Confessional in *UPB* (II), pp. 266–271.

7. Wordsworth, "It is a Beauteous Evening, Calm and Free."

8. Wordsworth, "To My Sister" (italics mine).

9. B'rachot, 9th Chapter, 54 a. I have benefited in the preparation of this section from discussions with Dr. Eugene Mihaly, Hebrew Union College–Jewish Institute of Religion, Cincinnati, Ohio.

10. Commenting on Psalm 69:14, ". . . let my prayer be unto Thee, O Lord, in an acceptable time, . . ." the Rabbis taught (B'rachot 8 a), "When is the time acceptable? When the congregation is praying."

11. *Tales of the Hasidim*, p. 150.

12. B'rachot 8 a. In addition to "praying," the individual must also study Torah and perform works of charity.

13. Leviticus 22:32. See B'rachot 21 b.

14. *UPB*, p. 118 (italics mine).

CHAPTER VIII

1. "The Philosophy Implicit in the Midrash," HUC Annual, Vol. XXVII, 1956, p. 251, by Dr. Henry Slonimsky.

2. Leviticus 19:2.

3. *Tales of the Hasidim,* p. 149.

4. The pamphlet, "Prayer," Dr. Henry Slonimsky, p. 16.

5. *Belief Unbound*, pp. 6, 7, as quoted by Dr. H. Slonimsky, "Prayer," p. 15.

6. Dr. H. Slonimsky, "Prayer," p. 18.